A WORLD OVERTURNED

A WORLD OVERTURNED

A BURMESE CHILDHOOD
1933–47

|✳|

Maureen Baird-Murray

CONSTABLE · LONDON

First published in Great Britain 1997
by Constable and Company Limited
3 The Lanchesters, 162 Fulham Palace Road
London W6 9ER
Copyright © Maureen Baird-Murray 1997
The right of Maureen Baird-Murray to be identified
as the author of this work has been asserted by her
in accordance with the Copyright, Designs and Patents Act 1988
ISBN 0 09 476400 X
Set in Monophoto Garamond by
Servis Filmsetting Ltd, Manchester
Printed in Great Britain by
St Edmundsbury Press Ltd
Bury St Edmunds, Suffolk

A CIP catalogue record for this book
is available from the British Library

CONTENTS

List of Illustrations · vii

Acknowledgements · viii

Map of Burma · ix

1   A Sweet-Pea World · 1

2   St Agnes's Convent · 9

3   Sugar-Cane Days · 19

4   Travels with Father · 35

5   Something Disastrous · 45

6   Enter the Japanese · 57

7   Under the Rising Sun · 65

8   Learning to Adjust · 73

9   Living with the Nuns · 81

10   Tea Parties and Daily Chores · 93

CONTENTS

11   Nuns and Guns · 105

12   Liberation and Farewell · 119

13   The Reading of a Will · 129

14   I Discover my Family · 139

15   Out into the Wide World · 149

16   Mr Ogden's Rangoon · 155

17   Going Home · 163

18   Going Back · 169

Glossary · 179

[vi]

LIST OF ILLUSTRATIONS

between pages 86 and 87

1 My parents
2 My father's work
3 Childhood
4 School
5 My grandparents' village
6 St Agnes Convent
7 'The men in my life' (age 12)
8 Ireland

The photographs of tribal people in plate 2 were taken by my father;
the photographs in plate 5 were taken by James Wickham

ACKNOWLEDGEMENTS

Alan Finch who showed an enthusiastic interest in my story from the very start and was a constant source of encouragement.

Anna Allott former professor of Burmese in the School of Oriental and African Studies, London, who translated the Burmese letter and took it on herself to rediscover some of my relations in Burma.

Margot Ogden for sharing some of her memories with me of life in pre-war Burma with her late husband, Roy Ogden.

Peggy Pastina (née West) who gave me an inkling of the perils faced by the fleeing families to India.

Andy (Holten Andersen) who most kindly gave me his report to the East Asiatic Company to use as I wish.

Margaret Body for her wise and sympathetic editing.

Carol O'Brien, editorial director of Constable, for her courteous and professional help.

Lastly but not least to James Wickham, also of Constable, my son-in-law, without whose help my story would not have been published.

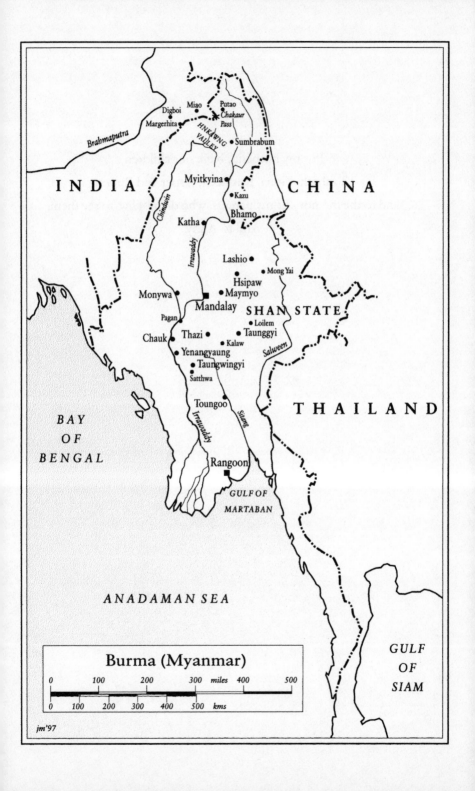

INDIA

CHINA

Brahmaputra

Digboi
Miao
Putao
Margerhita
Chakaur Pass
HNKAWNG VALLEY
• Sumbrabum

Myitkyina
• Kazu
Chindwin
Katha
Bhamo

Irrawaddy
Lashio •
• Mong Yai

Hsipaw
Monywa
Maymyo
Mandalay
SHAN STATE
Pagan
Chauk
Thazi
• Loilem
Taunggyi
• Kalaw
Yenangyaung
Salween
• Taungwingyi
Satthwa

Toungoo

Irrawaddy
Sittang

THAILAND

BAY
OF
BENGAL

Rangoon
GULF OF MARTABAN

ANADAMAN SEA

GULF
OF
SIAM

Burma (Myanmar)

| 0 | 100 | 200 | 300 *miles* | 400 | 500 |

| 0 | 100 | 200 | 300 | 400 | 500 *kms* |

jm'97

For my husband, Neil; our children,
Elizabeth, Fiona, Kathleen, Jasper and Rupert;
and to the memory of my parents, who did not live to see them.
And to Andy.

CHAPTER

|✳| 1 |✳|

A SWEET-PEA WORLD

MY BIRTH CERTIFICATE states that I was born in Mongyai in the Northern Shan States on 18 April 1933, that my father was Edward Wrixon Rossiter, nationality Irish, religion Church of Ireland, occupation Assistant Superintendent, Burma, and my mother was Khin Nyun Rossiter, nationality Burmese, religion Buddhist. My father had set sail for a career in the Burma Frontier Service in 1927 as an adventurous young man of twenty-three. At that time the country was governed as a province of India, and the main task of the Burma Frontier Service was to administer the rugged borders with China which were inhabited by hill peoples. There were Kachins, Padaungs, Thaundhus, Palaungs, Lahus, Was and many, many more tribes, but easily the greatest in number were the Shans. At the time I was born my father was Assistant Superintendent in Lashio.

There were thirty-two Shan States, covering a total area of some 56,000 square miles. When Burma was annexed by Britain in 1885, it included the Shan States which accordingly became British colonial territory, organised under feudal princes or *sawbwas*. There was never an invasion by the British, which probably accounts for why the British and the Shans got on extremely well together.

But my mother was Burmese. Her family were poor peasant folk from Taungdwingyi in the dry zone of Central Burma. A letter written to me by one of her brothers, very much later than the events in this story, curiously puts her as coming 'between sixth and seventh' in a family of eleven. Surprisingly, only two of this large family did not survive early childhood.

It was while my father was on tour and passing through Taungdwingyi that he stopped at a cheroot factory and caught sight of my mother. Struck by her beauty, he made several attempts to engage her in conversation, but it was to no avail as she kept running away to her mother, for she spoke no English and stood in some awe of the foreigner. My father, however, was not easily deflected, spoke fluent Burmese, as well as Shan and several dialects of the hill tribes. All his direct efforts being in vain, he had to have recourse to the headman of my mother's village to make the necessary arrangements for a meeting. This must have been something of a success because eventually permission was given for a marriage to take place, but not before certain conditions were set out by his future mother-in-law who struck a hard bargain. These were that my father would undertake the schooling of the younger children and that my mother was to be allowed home for one whole month every year. I do not know whether my mother had any say in this arrangement, but it would certainly have been a great feather in her parents' caps to have a daughter marry someone in the British ruling and occupying class.

I have in my possession a copy of their marriage certificate, stating that their marriage was solemnised at Mandalay on 22 April 1930 in the Office of the Senior Marriage Registrar, Mandalay, my father's age being given as 'Full', and that of my mother as 'Minor'. However it is probable that a Burmese marriage ceremony took place two or three years before this date.

My own earliest memories start in Loilem in the Southern Shan States. We lived in a large low wooden house on a brick foundation which was covered by nasturtiums. A narrow verandah surrounded most of it and was connected to the cookhouse by a roofed path, but it was otherwise open to the elements on both sides. I think we must have had plenty of sweet peas as well, for the sight and smell of sweet peas always bring my mind back to Loilem with a jolt. I remember it as a happy place where I spent many hours playing in a stream which ran through the compound. Years later I was to learn that no such stream existed – it was purely an open rainwater drain, but to me then it was a river.

My parents are there, but they are hazy figures, a tall stern-looking man in khaki shorts with green eyes, and my mother, petite and graceful, wearing a *longyi*, the Burmese version of the sarong, with a close-fitting jacket or blouse called an *eingyi*. And there are flowers in her hair, always jasmine. As though in a dream there is sometimes a little playmate with me, flitting in and out like a shadow. Together we look for a ball lost in a bed of nasturtiums and come across some caterpillars, huge, hairy and grotesquely coloured which brush our hands. Terrified, we run to the house where soothing balm is massaged to relieve the stinging.

On another occasion my little friend is screaming as a snake slithers towards her. My father shoots it with his gun, holding it up hanging lifeless over the barrel for us to see that it can no longer do us any harm. After that her shadow completely fades away. This little playmate never has a name, nor have I, but I do remember that my father is called 'Sir' or 'Master', in Burmese '*Thakin*', my mother 'Mistress' or '*Thakin Ma*' and I was '*Thakin Ma Le*', meaning 'Little Mistress'. We had servants who made a great pet of me and called me 'Baby Le', or little baby.

When my little friend disappeared my parents seemed to disappear with her. I am now in a wooden house, also with a verandah and with people who are not my parents, but nice, kind, smiling people. I now have a lovely red tricycle on which I ride constantly forwards and backwards on the verandah. As it were yesterday I recall an accident where my right foot got caught in the pedal, removing most of my big toe nail, leaving it hard and horny to this day. Vividly, I remember looking out on the road, really nothing more than a wide hard-baked track and seeing it covered in snakes. Short and white, rather like giant maggots, they hold me mesmerised, unable to move, until someone scoops me up and carries me away.

Another memory is that of drowning. There is an immense river, the opposite shore of which is barely visible. A lot of women are bashing clothes on the rocks or washing their children in the river while I play at its edge. Suddenly I lose my footing and must surely drown, but once again someone is there to clutch me out of the water just in time.

These last two events took place in Monywa, then a thriving village on the Chindwin river, quite a distance west from Mandalay. Here the people were rather darker-skinned than in Loilem, for I was now in a place where a great deal of trading was carried on with Indians. I was aware that the people looking after me were not my parents but I was quite happy, even though my parents and my little friend seemed to be away for such a long time.

And then my parents were back, just by themselves, and we returned to Loilem once more. But there was no little friend and, lacking the company of other children, I spent a lot of time in the servants' quarters, petted and spoiled as ever. There I watched the hill people who came regularly to sell vegetables and rice, sweet potatoes and other produce. They sat on their hunkers, dressed mostly in black, their sturdy legs encased in thin silver bands with yet more silver adorning their bodies. They spoke a strange language which was not Burmese, but I was used to a mixture of languages by now, for my parents and I spoke in Burmese to each other and to the servants, while my father had many British friends coming and going all the time whose language my mother and I found incomprehensible. As well as the civil servants and Public Works Department engineers there would be tea planters, foresters, Burmah Oil Company staff and employees of Steel Brothers, a well established British company trading in commodities such as cotton, petroleum, rice, rubber and teak. These people usually arrived in motor cars, stayed a while, then might take my father away with them for a few days, sometimes for much longer. In his absences he particularly relied on a man whom I remember thinking of as being Indian, who was probably his chief clerk.

As time went on I was aware of a change coming over my parents. My father's looks grew more stern and set, while my mother frequently appeared to be crying, but I did not know the cause of this change. Then one day the three of us got into the car and drove away from the house and Loilem. The destination was Kalaw, another town in the Southern Shan States. As I see it on the map today the distance does not appear great, but at the time I was sure that it was a long journey, lasting three days, stopping at night with friends. Not much was spoken during the journey; my father serious and stern, my mother quietly dabbing her eyes. Not an inkling did I have of what was in store for me.

At last we approached enormous iron gates and drove through them. On one side was a high bank cut into terraces on which grew a profusion of beautiful tall flowers. A huge eucalyptus tree stood at the end of the gravel drive and here we came to a stop in front of a low dark timber building with the customary verandah, but very much wider than I was used to, and stone-floored. There was little time to take in more of the surroundings for almost as soon as we stepped out of the car a door opened out of the low building and a figure, quite unlike anything I had ever seen before, came to greet us. She was dressed entirely in black from neck to foot and wore a starched white bonnet tied under her chin with long tabs reaching to her waist. The impression was that of a crow, a very old black crow, although her face was white with a lot of wrinkles and a couple of large moles. She tried to smile encouragingly at me but, still terrified, I gripped my mother's hand even tighter. The black robed figure and my father carried on a conversation in English of which neither my mother nor I understood a word.

After a while, to my surprise we were joined by a Burmese lady who was dressed just like my mother and they carried on a conversation in Burmese. Then turning to me, she asked if I would like to go for a little walk with her. Not wanting to leave

[6]

my mother, I shook my head. In the distance I could hear the voices of children at play.

'Wouldn't you like to go and see the other children?' she coaxed, to which I replied, 'No.' Then, producing some sweets, she held them out to me and repeated the invitation.

Won over by the sweets and curious to see what the children were doing, without a backward glance at my mother, I took the Burmese lady's hand as she led me up some wide smooth stone steps. Looking back it seems to me that the whole of that terrible day is forever linked to those wide smooth stone steps. The children's voices were getting nearer and nearer. It must have been playtime, for a great many children were in the playground, some very dark-skinned with jet black hair, others fairhaired with pink and white faces, boys and girls, all dressed identically, the boys in khaki shorts, the girls in navy blue tunics and white blouses. Some were on swings and see-saws and there seemed to be a lot of running games. Dotted here and there were the same crow-black robed figures, and it was when I saw these that my uneasiness returned, for I suddenly realised my mother was not with me. Turning to the Burmese lady, I said firmly that I wanted to go back to my mother. Smiling, she led me down the steps only just in time to see my parents driving away. In frantic desperation I broke away from her, running to catch up with the car, but it kept driving on with my parents looking straight ahead.

Unbelieving, stunned and frightened, I watched till it disappeared from view, then screaming and crying with disbelief, I turned and faced the black figures, for by now the place seemed to be full of them. Their attempts to take me gently by the hand and distract me failed completely, for I was kicking and hitting out in all directions. In the end they were too much for me, and four of them carried me to the playground where I was soon surrounded by jeering children. This then was my introduction to St Agnes's Convent English High School for Girls, Kalaw. It was also the last time that I was ever to see my parents together, a day I remember as if it were yesterday.

CHAPTER

|*|*| 2 |*|*|

ST AGNES'S CONVENT

ST AGNES'S CONVENT was founded by Italian nuns to educate girls of all ages, and boys up to about the age of ten. Teaching was in English, with Burmese as the second language. It was open to all denominations, irrespective of race or colour, so long as the fees could be paid. Kalaw was a hill station, that is to say one of four locations on the Shan plateau with a European type of climate, very pleasant for most of the year and reasonably tolerable during the rainy season. There were three seasons, a dry and hot season, a rainy season and a cool season. Always in the distance were the lofty blue hills reaching to a height of some 5000 feet above sea level. In the cool season especially the air was fresh and bracing with a keen bite in it, January's cherry blossoms making a magical painted carpet. The frosty nights and keen sunny days of March gave way to the hot season which lasted until the breaking of the monsoon in mid-May. But Kalaw was never unbearable, even at its hottest, because of the cool mountain breezes which brought a pleasant relief. It was therefore a favourite place for the wives and children of the administrative services and their men when on leave. Fruit in abundance grew everywhere in Kalaw, guavas, pomelos, oranges, limes, pineapples, mangoes, plums, durians, marians, bananas, as well as flowers in profusion. Exotic lilies, which I was later always to associate with catafalques and Requiem Masses, bloomed in the valleys and tiny blue flowers carpeted the woods, making a paradise of tranquil beauty. There were pine trees, eucalyptus, tamarind and jacaranda, as well as bamboo, maize and vegetables of all kinds. It had good roads and a rail connection to Thazi from which it was linked to all the main towns from Rangoon in the south to the very north at Myitkyina.

To this paradise came the nuns of the Order of the Redemption, probably in the 1920s, building their convent, starting with just one timber dwelling. Without exception all came from the north of Italy, some of them only learning English on the long sea voyage. Motivated by a strong and sincere zeal to convert souls to Christ and Catholicism through education, they worked hard, and by the time of my arrival in March 1938, some weeks before my fifth birthday, a great sprawl of buildings had been erected. There was a boys' dormitory, babies' (that is to say children of my age), middle girls' and senior girls' dormitories. There was also a dormitory for female teachers and the nuns' quarters.

My introduction into school was not a happy one and deserves to be passed over with as little lingering as possible. I had arrived in the morning wearing an ordinary child's dress in the European style but almost at once I was thrust into a school uniform of navy blue tunic and white blouse. Half dragged, half led by the hand of one of the frightening nuns and still unable to keep back my sobs, I was shown into the kindergarten, a large airy classroom under the boys' dormitory. On either side of a wide aisle were rows and rows of little desks at which sat little girls identically dressed to me and small boys in khaki shorts. Mechanically I tried to copy what the other children did, but as I was still unable to hold back my tears progress was very limited and my tears only resulted in the other children giggling and pointing their fingers at me. They were not all English, yet everyone seemed to be speaking such a strange language of which I had no understanding. Several of the children looked just like me with brown faces and short dark hair, cut in Japanese fashion, yet they would not speak Burmese which was all I could understand.

Never having been to a school nor even heard of one, I had no idea that I was in such a place, nor why. At recreation time we had a different playground to the one I had seen earlier and outside I could see the road down which my parents had gone in such a strange and frightening way. I must have made a mental note of the fence separating the school from the road and I don't remember quite when it was that I made my first attempt to run away. The school employed a lot of *malis* (gardeners or handymen) and I had made but short progress before one of them, recognising my uniform, brought me back to the nuns. They were terribly cross with me and, tying my hands behind my back, put me facing the corner of the babies' dormitory with the key turned in the lock. I don't know how long this punishment lasted but I did not give up. I had seen another part of the convent grounds where purveyors of forbidden foodstuffs sold their wares to the senior girls. This seemed a much better bet because the nuns seldom went there, which was why the senior girls picked this spot for their clandestine purchases. It was easy to slip out undetected when everyone's attention was occupied and I had made my way almost to the Kalaw Hotel when one of the servants, recognising my uniform, once again marched me back to the school. This time I received a caning on the backs of my legs as well as being tied and locked up.

Knowing no English did not help and any other language was strictly forbidden. As a result I did not know what was required of me and spent hours standing on a chair wearing a dunce's cap and being mocked by the other children. Not knowing whether I would ever see my parents again was unbearable, and retreating into my shell I soon gained a reputation for being stupid. My two unsuccessful attempts at escaping, with the resulting punishments, totally crushed my spirits; a dumb wretchedness came over me and now I really became so sullen that I was relegated to the bottom of the class, making no progress. There were one or two others who fared just as badly in class, though they did not try to run away. One was a little girl called Lennie Montgomery, and out of our common misery we drew comfort from each other. I gradually became accustomed to the taunts of the other children and I took no notice of them, so that little by little they ignored me – a merciful relief.

We were mostly in great awe of the big girls, but one of them, an Indian called Rosie Verma, had a way with the smaller children. She would take me by the hand, tell me to shut my eyes and promise to lead me into fairyland. A little walk with my eyes screwed shut would end with her saying, 'Here we are, this is fairyland', and I would open my eyes to find maybe a little circle of sweets arranged on the ground for me.

There were a few other bright spots, the brightest of all being the discovery of music. Regularly during the week we had song and action classes, and how very much I enjoyed them. Sitting at a piano on a revolving stool which looked quite unequal to the task of supporting her, sat Sister Amalia, grotesquely fat like one of the seven dwarfs in Snow White, with tomato-red pendulous cheeks and several chins. I was at first gripped with a dread that the stool would concertina to the ground under her weight, but once I got over that fear it was easy to lose myself in beautiful melodies which opened up a new world to me. Some of the tunes were accompanied by words, but in others we were made to go through a routine using handkerchiefs or brilliantly painted Burmese parasols which looked so pretty as we twirled and fluttered them in time to the music that for a time I forgot how unhappy I was. I longed for these classes, the only ones in which I could take part without the need to understand what was said to me.

Then there were the walks to St James' Woods. These were just beyond the great iron-gated school entrance, and we were taken there in crocodile formation by two nuns. But once there, we were allowed to roam within hailing distance. Harebells grew in abundance, so did wild lilies, white and orange. But what caught my eye by the brilliance of their colouring were the many beetles and insects which flitted from branch to branch, the lustre of their dainty wings ever changing as the sun glinted on them. Very soon I was doing what the others were doing, catching a few to take back to the dormitory. We used empty cardboard packaging that came with toothpaste or ink bottles, and with a few holes inserted in the sides for air, and green leaves for food, we kept them alive for days and days.

Another favourite pastime was playing with mud. The soil in the playground was clayish and it was possible to make rough models of people, animals and houses. Trapped water in the base of trees enabled us to make tiny dams and streams and we tried to copy pictures in books to make models of windmills, trees and bridges.

So very gradually I was resigned to this new life, although longing so much for my parents and wondering if I would ever see them again. One day stands out in the memory, the day a parcel arrived for me. It was unwrapped by one of the nuns in the classroom, all of us crowding around her, and to everyone's delight it revealed a Shirley Temple doll. About a foot in height, with eyes that opened and shut, a mass of fair ringlets, the hem of an exquisite dress attached to her wrists by blue ribbons, it was the most marvellous thing I had ever seen. I wanted to take it out of its glass case, but as I reached out I was stopped by the nun before I could touch it. She pointed out that it was too fragile to handle but that it would be left on the shelf for all to see and admire on Sundays and holidays, adding that it was a present from my father for my fifth birthday. Even though I did not know what a birthday meant it was astounding news for it indicated that my father was somewhere around and I hugged the knowledge to myself all day. But then I went back to asking myself why he and my mother had left me in this wretched place, and when I would ever see them again. The arrival of the parcel made a great difference in the way I was regarded, and for the time being anyway, I was spared the dunce's cap, or standing on chairs for everyone's derision. Gradually, too, I began to understand some English and make friends.

I fell into the school routine without too much difficulty, although going to Mass almost daily was somewhat of an ordeal. Getting up in the mornings to the harsh ringing of the great brass bell, then being helped into the uniform and laced or buttoned shoes was not easy. When I first came to the convent I had no idea how to dress myself as an *ayah* had always looked after me at home and all I had to do was to stretch out my foot and demand that she put my shoe on! This is where another hazy memory refuses to come into complete focus. But at that early age at school I actually had my own personal servant still, a first cousin on my mother's side called Sein Shan who was there to look after me, in return for which she received an education, in accordance with my father's promise when he married my mother. Because I had not yet met any of my mother's vast family and because she was three years older than me, Sein Shan was just another new stranger, but because she was not a grown up she was not so frightening. She didn't clout me with sharp knuckles while brushing the tangles out of my hair as the adult servants assigned to the babies' dormitory invariably did. I wish I could remember more about her then. Hair had to be brushed three times a day, morning, evening and at the end of classes before tea. Fortunately all the servants spoke Burmese which made it easier to understand what was required.

Mass was said in the church across the road by an Italian priest, Father Boldrini. He had a very fair complexion, sparkling blue eyes and a flowing white beard which terrified me, especially when the smoke from his cigarettes wafted through it. Monsters in Burmese colouring books always had beards. Parrot-fashion we repeated the prayers and responses of the Mass in English and Latin, not understanding a word of either, but the hymns were tuneful and we did the best we could to show that we knew all the words. Kneeling on the hard benches was pure purgatory, making our knees sore and red but luckily the little ones did not have to stay right to the end of Mass.

Every Thursday Mass was said in the convent's own chapel, so we did not have to get up quite so early then.

Recalling what a varied background of races and religions the children came from, the nuns really excelled themselves when it came to meals. Every single dietary rule was observed, and so the variety of meals served was enormous – not just fish meals or meat meals, but fish-with-scales meals, fish-without-scales meals, porkless meals, all-vegetable meals, milkless meals and so on. We were attended at table by Burmese and Indian waiters. On Sundays and holy days the Burmese waiters donned very fine *gaungbaungs* (a turban-like head-dress) in brilliant pinks, greens and gold, and wore gay *longyis* and plain jackets, while the Indians, very smart in their white jackets and trousers, sported flowing turbans, sometimes embellished with sparkling brooches. Grace before and after meals was always said, and chairs had to be drawn and replaced quietly, sometimes over and over again until the supervising nun was satisfied. Once seated, five minutes silence had to be observed and in this period the waiters fastened starched table napkins round the necks of the little ones and the food was served. Then a noisy chatter would break out, accompanied by the clanging of cutlery as some of us learnt to grapple with knives and forks for the first time. Teatime, always preceded by a wash and brush-up in the dormitories, was the only meal where we actually ate bread and butter which we did not much like. At all other meals rice was served, even at breakfast, although on Sundays in the cool season we had lovely rusks which we were allowed to dunk into our hot steaming mugs of cocoa, frequently replenished by the waiters. The refectory was normally a place of happy relaxation – except for one custom. When a boy had behaved particularly badly the punishment consisted of a public caning in the middle of the refectory before the start of the meal, stunning us all into a frightened silence for the greater part of the meal.

Besides Lennie Montgomery, my other particular friend was a boy called Richard Saon Pha, the son of a *sawbwa*. As princeling heads of large districts in the Shan States, *sawbwas* could have more than one wife and many sent their children to the convent for the cachet of an English education. For the most part these children got on well together but sometimes when quarrels arose one child would proclaim that her mother was the *mahadevi* (chief wife), while that of her opponent was only a minor wife.

I cannot remember how long it was after I had been left at school, but one day Richard returned from the boys' closets to the classroom determined to catch my eye. I knew that he had something to tell me.

'Your mother's in the parlour and she's asking for you,' he whispered excitedly.

Gathering all my courage, for I was afraid to speak to any nun, I put up my hand for permission to speak, intending to ask to go to the girls' closets, the only reason allowed for leaving the classroom. But anticipating a refusal, I decided not to wait for permission and instead raced headlong in the direction of the parlour.

She was there. With outstretched arms she ran towards me and enfolding me, rocked me to and fro while I shed uncontrolled tears of relief and happiness, mingled with reproaches. It was a wonderful, unforgettable moment and, clinging to her like a leech, I would not let her go. Soon her tears gave way to a grudging approval as, holding me at arm's length, she scrutinised my uniform and my general well-being and seemed fairly satisfied. It was not the end of term however, so her intention

[17]

to take me out practically paralysed the administration. Mother
Superior frowned on her visit and the Burmese teacher was
summoned to translate her disapproval, but it made not the
slightest impression on my mother. I took a tight defiant hold
of my mother's hand and, secure in her presence, watched the
outcome of the struggle between her and Mother Superior with
mounting excitement. The latter, probably realising that she
was up against an immovable force, reluctantly gave way and
allowed us out for the day. Remembering that day so long ago
still makes me smile today as, quietly jubilant, we trotted off on
foot to spend our time together. We bought a pair of sandals
for me and lots of sweets and biscuits to take back. The day was
heaven and when it was time to return in the evening my mother
could not bear to leave me there and insisted on staying.

There was consternation among the nuns, for this was a most
unusual state of affairs. But my mother had no understanding
of European educational customs. She refused to go, so what
were they to do with her? Resignedly, the poor nuns capitulated
and had a bed made up for her in the teachers' dormitory. With
wide-eyed interest she watched the bedtime routine and, imi-
tating the servants, brushed my hair and folded my clothes on
the bedside chair as they did. It was only after night prayers were
said, the mosquito nets drawn down and I had been well tucked
in that she was content to withdraw to the teachers' quarters.
Over the next couple of days she placed herself where she
could see me either in the classroom or the babies' dormitory.
The nuns disapproved but were impotent, while my mother
ignored or chose not to understand their disapproval and
embarrassment. School lost some of its terror and hardship for
me, and when she finally left I was secure in the knowledge that
I would be seeing her again at the end of term.

CHAPTER

|✳|✳| 3 |✳|✳|

SUGAR-CANE DAYS

THE DAYS PASSED quickly after my mother's visit and it was soon the end of term. She came by herself to take me to her home village for the school holidays and, walking the long road to Kalaw station we caught the train to Sat-thwa. It was a lengthy journey, not entirely because the distance was great, but because whenever the train stopped at a station it did so for hours. Chinese and Burmese food-sellers, carrying enormous containers balanced on long rods over their shoulders, ran up and down the train shouting out their wares. Delicious curries and rice, fried sparrows skewered on bamboo sticks, sugar-cane circles and water melon wedges. A particularly pungent delicacy was a purplish, sticky rice baked in the hollow of bamboo lengths and eaten moulded into a ball, dipped in sesame oil and salt. Food was placed on glistening banana leaves and eaten straight away in one's fingers. Beggars, mostly Indians, thronged the station, some sleeping on thin mattresses which could be rolled up when they had to move on. It was immensely exciting and colourful, and going to sleep on a top bunk was a new experience. Next day we arrived at Sat-thwa, a village in Central Burma, about five miles from Taungdwingyi. This was my mother's home and I was about to meet my maternal grandparents for the first time.

We got off the train on a hot blistering day, me still in my uniform of navy blue gym slip, white blouse and topee. Everything was dry, hard baked and white from the fierce heat of the sun, the plain before us immensely flat and featureless, the sky wide and open. We were on a tarmac road on one side of which I noticed a substantial wooden house with a real English-style garden. Only the well-to-do owned wooden houses and in this one lived two Burmese ladies whom we were to visit once or twice later. Soon we turned on to a dusty white track and passed a large banyan tree. On one of its branches was an offering of food to the *nats*, or spirits. In hushed tones my mother explained that we were always to go in fear when we saw one of these trees as some of the *nats* were very evil and could do terrible, harmful things. Indeed, if we passed a much bigger banyan tree it would sometimes have a circle of candles burning around it to propitiate the *nats* because it was believed that the bigger the tree, the more malignant the resident *nats*. It was not just banyans, they inhabited all sorts of places, waterfalls, some river banks and even rocks and mountain tops. She made it all sound very frightening.

The white dust rose as we walked and the intense heat made my hair stick to my head and the elastic chin strap of my topee became uncomfortable. There was not a dwelling in sight, but just as I had begun to wonder if the road was ever going to end there rose up in front of us a long bamboo fence which went on as far as the eye could see on either side of the dusty track and encircled the entire village. Through an opening in the fence we came on a collection of single-storey bamboo huts built on long poles about fifteen feet or so off the ground. No proper roads existed, but the rows of houses were intersected by dusty tracks all looking exactly the same. Long before reaching our house we had gathered up a bunch of curious children, mystified by the arrival of the strange newcomer so oddly dressed. Some were covered in running sores, others, the bigger ones, had babies strapped to their backs, while a few carried earthen water pots on their heads. It was with difficulty that my mother kept the more curious from taking too close an interest in me, and we were glad to reach the house where my grandparents were waiting.

The entrance was approached by a rickety flight of stairs, having the dubious benefit of a none too secure rail for support. This led to a verandah about ten feet wide with railings and a floor of thin strips of bamboo. At one end stood a kerosene oil drum used to catch rain water, with a coconut shell ladle dangling down one side of it. Stepping over a lintel about a foot high, we entered the main part of the dwelling. In one corner two thin mattresses were propped up ready to be unrolled at night for my grandparents. Stepping over another high lintel and down a step brought us to the kitchen where the cooking was done in a large boxed area on three raised brick piles. Earthenware pots (*chatties*) of varying sizes lined one wall next to a water drum. An area sectioned off by bamboo matting served as a bathroom, complete with water drum and coconut shell scoops. From the living room a door led into a bedroom for my mother and me. There was a large wooden bed with four posts for holding up the mosquito net and a dressing table with a long oval mirror. I think it would be safe to say that we had the only bed in the village. Apart from a low table around which we sat on our hunkers for meals, that was the extent of the furniture. High up in one corner of the main room was a sort of altar and ever present offerings for the *nats*.

Nobody had heard of bathrooms or closets. You either sluiced yourself down with water on the verandah, modestly covered by a *longyi*, but in full view of passers-by who would share the gossip of the day with you while you bathed or, if you required privacy, you went to the partitioned area off the kitchen. A very basic latrine stood at the far end of the compound. There were no curtains, sofas or chairs, but we were very comfortable and happy.

It would be hard to say just what the people of Sat-thwa did for a living. There must have been about five hundred people in the village all selling foodstuffs and firewood to each other, or building houses for one another. There was a school two or three doors away from our house and a monastery (*phongyi kyaung*) on the outskirts. Even in those days there was a relatively high rate of literacy, for monastic schools were generally available in almost every village throughout the country and open to all Buddhist youths or boys, who went there for a period of one or two years to learn the rudiments of their faith and receive an education. Girls also had a basic schooling in Burmese. Private fee-paying mission schools taught only in English, and these afforded the easiest entrance to colleges.

The better off villagers drove bullock-carts, one or two had a horse and cart which plied to and from Taungdwingyi, some cut sugar-cane, but there were no paddy-fields or cultivation of ground-nuts. Nor can I remember any shops. But there was a market every five days, when ear-piercing and tattooing took place. People carried out their chores in leisurely, unhurried fashion. There was always a great deal of activity at the village's four wells and fetching water consumed the greater part of the day. Always performed by the young girls and women, with pots balanced gracefully on their heads on coils of cloth, it gave ample opportunity for mild flirtation with the young gallants who hung around hoping for just such an opportunity. Almost every day as night fell the plaintive calls of mothers rose from their verandahs, as they waited impatiently for the return of their dallying daughters. It was at the village well also that the women washed their clothes, beating them on the rocks, helping each other with the wringing and spreading them on the stones to dry. Here also they sometimes washed their long dark hair, using a thick slithery liquid made from the bark of the thayaw tree as shampoo. Little children not quick enough to escape their mothers would also be subjected to a merciless scrubbing.

In this village I spent some of the happiest times of my childhood. Nothing in the way of chores was required of me, although I longed to be allowed to fetch water from the well. But my mother was a bit of a snob in her own way. She liked the homage paid to her as the wife of a foreign official, setting her apart from the rest of village. Manual labour in Burmese eyes was degrading, certainly not done by white people or by children of white people. This also applied to ear-piercing. I begged in vain to have my ears pierced, so that I could wear some of mother's lovely earrings, even though I would not have been allowed to wear them in school. But while this would have been in order for my little cousins, my mother knew that it was definitely not the thing for a child boasting a white father.

[23]

So I played all day long with the village children who unlike me, had more than a few chores to get on with, and who often came to play with babies almost as big as themselves strapped on their backs. When the games became more demanding, the babies would be unstrapped and allowed to roam freely amongst the pigs and hens, to be hastily strapped back when we heard a particular child's name being called by its parent. No sooner had one child been called back than another would appear complete with baby sister or brother strapped on her back. At first I was rather perplexed by the names given to some of my playmates, such as Kwe-Ma, literally Bitch or worse. But I came to understand that these were protective names designed to disguise the fact that the parents hoped the girls, in particular, would grow up into raving beauties or have untold good fortune in later years. As at the convent, we played with mud which we scooped up into a mound, made a dimple in the peak of the mound with our elbows, spat into it, covered it up with a fine sprinkling of dust, and there, magically, was a cake or biscuit for sale. For money we used broken bits of crockery or watermelon seeds. Walking on stilts was also popular for those who could persuade their fathers to make them, otherwise we improvised with empty tin cans pierced at one end through which was threaded a piece of twine gripped with our toes.

My convent holidays did not coincide with those of the village school and in the daytime while lessons were in progress I hung around the entrance waiting for my friends to come out. I could hear them as they sang out their multiplication tables in Burmese, parrot-fashion. Just inside the gate a woman had installed herself with an enormous wok, stirring delicious smelling fritters made of calabash, whilst on a flat griddle next to it some delicate transparent pancakes were cooking. Once or twice the headmistress, catching sight of me, made it quite plain that she neither liked me nor approved of my upbringing in a foreign school, and as for my mother marrying a foreigner – here she used a derogatory term which translates as chicken droppings!

The village children wore *thanahka* on their faces in big round circles on their cheeks and sometimes on their foreheads. This was a paste made by grinding small lengths of a special tree on a stone slab. When mixed with water it produced a pleasant smelling and soothing paste which some people claimed warded off mosquitoes, protected the skin from the sun and kept it nice. They also knotted their hair into a topknot, sometimes sticking a slate pencil into it, but I was not allowed either of these customs and always wore a European type of dress.

No mention of my father was ever made and I don't think I was aware of his absence. My grandfather, U Shan Hpyu, with his waist-length hair coiled into a topknot, would smile sweetly at me, never having very much to say. His main job seemed to be collecting our firewood. Too poor to own his own bullock-cart, he would hire one occasionally and, as a great treat, take me out for the day to collect the wood. For such an outing my mother always dressed me in my school regulation bright green woollen bathing costume and made sure I wore my topee, for I was already brown enough she thought, and she did not want me to become any darker. With a tiffin-carrier containing our food for the day, grandfather and I would set out at the slowest pace imaginable, the bullocks swishing their tails in an attempt to keep the flies away, the wheels squeaking as they turned, and the whole atmosphere inducing drowsiness and peace. We hardly spoke, quietly enjoying each other's company. We would stop at a clearing by a large pond where he would set me down and he would then go a little way on foot and start chopping. The pond was covered in water lilies with exquisitely coloured dragonflies darting about which I would try and catch in vain. After a leisurely lunch he would lie down in the shade, then chop a bit more firewood, load up the bullock-cart and eventually return home. Flying kites was a favourite pastime and he would sometimes allow me to accompany him out of the village enclosure, deftly handling his delicate geometric-shaped kites and even occasionally allow me to stagger along under the weight of the huge heavy reels of cotton by which they were controlled.

My grandmother Daw Tha Mé ran the household and cooked the most delicious meals, the preparation of which (especially the mid-day meal) seemed to take up most of the morning. For all the spices, seeds, leaves and powders would have to be ground to a paste of the required consistency on her grinding stone. Her fish curries were particularly delicious, but whenever I asked the name of the fish she would say it was just 'river fish'. It was rare for a meal to be completed at one sitting for my friends were always calling me out to play. But the Burmese are very indulgent with their children, allowing them an uninhibited childhood, without care as far as is possible. They will not, however, put up with any disrespect shown to elders, and children learn from a very early age to *shiko* (corresponding to the Indian salaam or the Chinese and Japanese kowtow) if they have to cross the path of an adult. But again, I was not expected to do even this at home.

The games we played were often boisterous and my grandmother's lap was always ready for me to throw myself on to, either out of petulant tiredness or in a fit of pique at not getting my own way with my playmates. From the ceiling a hammock was suspended, another refuge from the heat of the day. Occasionally my grandmother required me to do her a small favour which was to work the fan above her as she rested at mid-day. At other times it was to walk on her as she lay down, which relieved the aches and pains in her joints, quite a common practice in Burmese villages. My simple loving and indulgent grandparents were one of my early childhood's strongest loves, and one which has never died.

As for my mother, I try to see her as others did, but I was so attached to her that I would fail. She was very pretty, pale and had a gentle, serene appeal, even when her face was in repose. Clothes, jewellery and pretty flowers were her delight and long was the time spent dressing her ankle-length hair. It was such a treat to be allowed to watch her getting ready to go out. She seemed to have three separate styles for doing her hair. For everyday it was coiled into a gentle knot on the nape of her neck, held in position with an ivory comb with a circlet of jasmine. For festive but informal occasions it would be wound into a topknot, but a loop of it was allowed to trail over one ear. For very formal affairs a great deal more attention had to be paid and some help from her mother or a friend enlisted as her hair would have to be coiled most carefully and smoothly on the top of her head in a sort of cylinder shape and kept in place with hairpins and ivory ornaments.

Hardly ever did I see her soil her hands with housework, as my grandmother took care of it all, but she did beautiful tatting and attended to the morning ritual of feeding the *phongyis*, the Buddhist monks who filed through the village with their black lacquer bowls. This was done to attain merit, for *phongyis* are required to cut themselves off from the world and to undertake no worldly tasks apart from that of educating the young. This

[27]

gave the *phongyis* merit and also anyone who supported them. Not allowed to own anything apart from their robes, they were nevertheless extremely influential and commanded a great deal of respect and veneration from the ordinary people. Their shaven heads, orange robes, palm-leaf fans and the obligatory alms bowls were a common sight. Sometimes they carried umbrellas and one could tell the rank of a *phongyi* just by looking at his umbrella. Yellow in colour, the ribs etched out in black, the longer and more numerous the ribs the more senior and important the *phongyi*.

My mother never spoke to me of my father, nor did I ask where he was. But frequently I noticed her opening a powder compact and as she looked into it tears would come into her eyes. In it there was a tinted photograph of a little girl, who was not me, but when I asked who she was and why she cried she would remain silent and shake her head sadly. For the first few days of the holidays I barely let her out of my sight, afraid she would disappear again. Jealously, I eyed anyone who came near her, sometimes pushing away whoever I thought came too close, for that was my place and no one else's. Sometimes one of her brothers stayed with us and, when he did so, he shared our bed, which was quite a normal practice in Burmese families. As he was also a favourite uncle I did not mind. Gradually, realising my fears were unfounded, I relaxed and spent more time with my playmates.

Occasionally we made a trip into Taungdwingyi, the nearest big town. This was usually in a cart drawn by a small Burmese horse which seemed too fragile for the task of pulling all the people who piled aboard. Once a group of villagers hired a taxi to take us to Taungdwingyi. A motor vehicle of any sort was a great novelty, everyone demanding a seat. There must have been at least a dozen or so crammed into it. But the journey was short lived for we soon attracted the attention of a policeman who made us all get out. Crestfallen, we had either to return to the village on foot, or make the rest of the journey into the town by pony cart.

I don't remember much about Taungdwingyi except that it was very crowded and that I had to dress up and put shoes on. It was regarded as quite an outing by my mother who loved making her way round the bazaars and shops. I preferred hanging round the sugar-cane crusher, watching the juice spurt out in a great rush, later to be made into jaggery, or large slabs of solid dark brown unrefined sugar. Sugar-cane grew like bamboo and when it was cut and taken in bullock-carts to the refining centres, the village urchins would follow behind stealing a length at a time, which was quite easy to do as bullocks walk so slowly. I loved joining these urchins and hung around while the cane was cut up into smaller lengths with big knives called *dahs* and distributed among the gang. What a sticky state we got into as the juice dribbled down our elbows and the fronts of our clothes, but it was exquisitely sweet and worth the mess, which could easily be sluiced off with water.

We seldom ventured farther than Taungdwingyi, although once we went on a long train journey to stay with some more of my mother's relations in a place called Chauk. This was a town on the Irrawaddy some hundred miles south-west of Mandalay. Arriving late in the evening, it was too dark to get any impression of our surroundings. Imagine my surprise next morning when looking out of the window I saw for the very first time enormous oil derricks rising out of the ground like steel monsters. For, of course, this was near Yenangyaung (literally 'oil stream'), the oilfields belonging to the Burmah Oil

Company, one of the major British commercial interests in the country. Burma in those days produced more oil for its size than any other country in the world, as I was later to find out from my geography books.

Several of my mother's family seemed to have settled in Chauk, probably employed by the oil company. There was Maung Than, whose wife had a stall in the market. The word *maung* denotes a younger brother. There was also a sister, Ma Hla Tin, who had married a goldsmith with a numerous family, and another sister Ma Htwa Hla who had returned to Chauk from Monywa. They all made a great fuss of me, fingered my dress and shoes and socks, the likes of which they had never seen before.

There was a very happy-go-lucky atmosphere in the village of Sat-thwa, children constantly going in and out of each other's houses without special invitation. While I was popping in and out of my friends' houses I once came upon preparations being made for a funeral. Fascinated, I watched as the mourners kept up a noisy wail, and could barely take my eyes away from the corpse, for her face had been grotesquely made up. My gaze travelled down to her feet which were bare and I saw that the big toes were bound together with a strand of hair. I wanted to know why this was done, but was afraid to ask, afraid also because we were all filled with the wildest superstitious dread of the dead.

Occasionally there were *pwes* or stage shows which usually lasted two or three days. For this a special stage would be erected under a shelter while the audience squatted on the ground, coming and going as they pleased, right into the early hours of the morning. As for the musicians, it was hard to tell where they sat as they sometimes mingled with the crowd, or at other times were hidden from the audience below the level of the stage, while all the time the selling of food and drinks went on without any heed to the play. Some of the crowd seemed to sleep right through the performance, with sleeping children in their laps.

What was happening on the stage was quite incomprehensible to me but there was much ribald laughter and everyone seemed highly entertained. The gorgeously attired performers in their winged tight-fitting jackets had me enthralled, and the clowns with their heavily applied and mask-like make-up frightened me rather, although everyone laughed a great deal at their jokes. Like the plays, the musical instruments were traditional, consisting of bamboo flutes, brass castanets and wooden clappers; there were drums of various kinds, some single, others hung several together on a bamboo frame but all played by one person. There were also triangular gongs hung on a single frame and struck with padded hammers. At every Burmese *pwe* there is also a boat-shaped instrument with bamboo keys of various thickness which give out mellow notes when struck by bamboo sticks.

Scenes of village life linger in my mind. The early morning vendors would call out their wares of fried sparrows on spits, boiled peas, *ngapi* (pressed rotten fish – very much an acquired taste), dried meat, puréed ants and sesame oil. Local youths pulling up their *longyis* and tucking the ends into the waist bands to get more freedom of movement, played *chin-lone* in the dusty road, causing the young girls to stop and stare at their agility in catching the hollow ball of woven cane with the backs of their heels or letting it travel down their shoulders and arms. Pariah dogs roamed the track, mangy and emaciated, hoping for a morsel to be thrown at them, instead of which they got a bucket of water. In the evenings, even in the hot season, women would gather round a fire and drink green tea, watching the embers glow, very often with sleeping children in their laps, while the men, inveterate gamblers all, would gather in the tea-shops, whittling away their hard-earned money.

Only once did anything happen to mar my blissful existence. My mother decided that she would go to Taungdwingyi for the day by herself. An icy thread of fear shot through me as I remembered that terrible first day at school in Kalaw, but my tears and pleas were to no avail. A pony cart was summoned and when I saw her disappear, I knew I would never see her again. Try as they would, my grandparents were unable to distract or comfort me, and at last, fearing for my well-being, they were forced to ask the police to look out for my mother and bring her back. It was late in the day when she returned. One look at my swollen, tear-stained face told her all. She was not angry, she simply picked me up, and my world was safe and wonderful once more. So my school holidays were spent in total bliss. Liberated from the rules which governed every minute of convent life, I ran wild.

It is hard to remember just how often I went home for the holidays. I know it was not every time because I can also remember staying at school when the numbers of children were greatly diminished, when rules were slightly relaxed and great picnics arranged. I also realise I went home at different seasons, for I have vivid memories of getting up on chilly mornings to find that my grandmother had lit a fire in the compound in front of the house, around which sat my family and friends wrapped in shawls and blankets. When I joined them my mother would dress me in front of the fire, warming the insides of my socks over the embers. It was on mornings like these that we would have a breakfast of the pungent purplish rice baked in bamboo which I had first seen at railway stations, my mother moulding it in her hand for me before dipping it in sesame oil and salt. Burma grows sixty or seventy types of rice and pounding it in a big wooden seesawing pestle and mortar contraption was a regular part of village life.

The dreaded day would at last arrive when my mother had to take me back to school. Knowing I had no wish to return, my little friends would hide me in their houses until the daily train had departed, and it was quite usual for me to be taken back to school two weeks late. Years after, the nuns were to tell me that this happened every term – my mother failing to understand why I had to be returned to school at all when there was a perfectly good Burmese school only two doors away from her parents' house. Admittedly, it was limited in what was taught and there would certainly be no English, all the pupils leaving well before their teens in order to make a contribution to the family funds. Many were the letters of complaint the nuns sent to my father about my late return to school, pointing out that I could hardly be expected to make any progress without my mother's co-operation. All perfectly true of course, for during the holidays I spoke only Burmese and forgot every word of English I had had such a struggle to learn during the preceding term. No wonder the nuns were exasperated.

It must have been during one of the last holidays in Sat-thwa that a noticeable change came over my mother. She grew somewhat serious in a way that reminded me of the last days at Loilem, and the chill of apprehension gripped me once more. Little things stand out, at the time not really significant, but taking on a significance years later. Could there be a connection with the little girl whose picture was in her compact, for she looked at it often, her eyes misting over. No longer did she spend happy hours trying on her lovely clothes and jewellery, nor did she hold her head up as high as she was accustomed to in the village.

She had begun working for the cheroot factory again. Boxes of them would arrive at our house, and she would deftly collect a hand-span of cheroots and place a brand strip round them before depositing them in another box ready for collection. People were giving us odd looks, they seemed less friendly, almost mocking and some even seemed to shun her altogether, she whose social position had undoubtedly been the greatest in the village. I didn't understand what was happening and wished I could protect her from the world she now found so hard. But what mattered most to me was that I was with her morning, noon and night, which was all I ever needed to keep me happy, even if I didn't quite understand all that was going on around us.

CHAPTER

|✳| 4 |✳|✳|

TRAVELS WITH FATHER

AFTER TWO YEARS in the kindergarten, aged about seven, I was put in the first standard. This was in the charge of Sister Seraphina, the most dreaded of all the nuns in the convent. Never in my life had I come across anything or anyone quite as terrifying as her. It was rumoured that before she became a nun she had been an actress, but that did not explain why she had transformed into such a monster. She would have made a good zealot as, foaming at the mouth, totally possessed by some demoniac force, she made effective use of cane, ruler and her right hand. And all because I could not speak English! Not understanding the language and therefore unable to do what was required of me sent her into a rage. In desperation I would throw out the odd word in English that I had retained during the holidays – most often the wrong word. This would so infuriate Sister Seraphina that she would lash out at me with her fists, hitting me with such force that it sometimes threw me to the other end of the room, making me temporarily deaf. I was not her only victim, but I was certainly the most favoured. Unable to stand up for myself and consumed with fear and misery, I did not attain even the minimal academic standard required.

Once again I was wretched and miserable, but once again there was someone or something to come to the rescue. In the kindergarten it had been the discovery of music; now it came in the human form of Sister Marie-Louise whose job it was to supervise the middle-sized girls' dormitory. This dormitory housed thirty to forty girls between the ages of seven and twelve. She managed us with the help of three or four Karen servant girls. Of all the tribes the Karens were the easiest to convert. This was because they believed that a lost book containing all the knowledge of their religion would one day be brought back to them by a white man. Karen children were often abandoned to the nuns in infancy, and brought up by them until suitable marriages could be arranged, or they themselves became nuns helping with the running of the kitchens or dormitories. Our dormitory ran like clockwork. We were now no longer babies and able to do almost everything for ourselves. Every morning we folded our bedclothes over our bedside chairs (for the bed to be remade by the servants), teeth, hair and nails were inspected, and morning prayers said (although ninety-nine per cent of the children were non-Christians), before we went to Mass. Twice a week we stood in line to receive a hateful dose of castor oil, holding a double fold of toilet paper under our chins. Twice a week before bedtime we stood by our beds waiting to be called to collect fresh clothing for the next day. Everything was beautifully tidy and clean.

It was for many of us the first introduction to WCs, electric lights, running water from taps, wash basins, toothbrushes and hot-water baths. When it was our day for having a bath we stood on the verandah and yelled for the *mali* to bring the hot water which he carried in two kerosene oil cans all the way from the kitchens. For us to go the kitchens ourselves was an expulsion offence. These *malis*, almost without exception Gurkhas, worked non-stop, at the beck and call of the nuns, and got little thanks from the children, for saying thank you to a servant was almost unheard of. But they were well off compared with the rest of the manual working class, well housed within the compound and allowed to have their families with them, to the envy of the less fortunate. The *mali* assigned to our dormitory was said to have killed another man in an argument, and it was only through the intervention of the nuns that he escaped hanging. They had enough faith in him to stand surety for him and he repaid their trust in every possible way. I see him now, his knees buckled with the weight of the cans, his thin sinewy legs and bare feet seeming far too spindly to cope with the burden they were carrying, yet seldom faltering, his neck veins bulging with the strain imposed by the heat and effort, and all the time a smile etched into his weatherbeaten face.

Bathing was a very modest and decorous affair. Donning *longyis*, four of us at a time, each in a zinc bathtub of water, scrubbed ourselves as best we could, while not revealing an inch of flesh from the shoulders down. Once a week the Karen girls went through our hair with fine toothcombs to make sure there were no foreign bodies. If any were found, treatment was most unpleasant – a dowsing with kerosene oil over the whole head, making one smell unbearably.

Every Thursday (the weekly holiday) we draped our bed-clothes over the balconies, mattresses as well, and gave them a good beating to get rid of dust and bugs, then helped each other to make up the beds. Mosquito nets also were given a good airing and replaced. Thursday was the day when the *dhobis* came. These were low caste washermen who never used soap except for washing clothes. Almost invariably Indian, they wore immaculately white turbans and *dhotis*, the traditional loose garb the ends of which are pulled up between the legs and fastened into the waist band. Our clothes were sorted in piles, then the long counting and recounting would commence, first in Hindustani by the *dhobis*, then in English by Sister Marie-Louise who kept an eagle eye on the proceedings, entering items and quantities in a long thick book, before the *dhobis* departed salaaming with their bundles. The same meticulous count was taken and recorded when they came back the following Thursday, the clothes beautifully clean, but often minus buttons from a merciless bashing on the rocks by the stream. It was a lucky thing that the Karens were such good needlewomen, able to repair the damage.

One night I was woken by a shake from Sister Marie-Louise who raised a finger to her lips to keep silence, and beckoned me to the dressing-room. This was a room which had a long white trough with cold water taps at regular intervals. Here we washed our faces and cleaned our teeth, collecting our sponges and tooth brushes from two long rows of lockers. Now displayed on the locker tops were some small everyday items such as pencils, books, marbles, slates, and a small pile of coins in rupees, annas and pice. Four pice made one anna, and sixteen annas made one rupee. Very patiently and with great gentleness Sister Marie-Louise played out a game with me, placing the small objects as though in a market stall and sending me to do the shopping. In no time at all I caught on and was thoroughly enjoying the intricacies of counting money, bringing back the change and understanding at last the purpose of learning by heart the multiplication tables up to twelve, plus the sixteen times table. We kept this up for a few more nights, sometimes changing to reading textbooks on geography or playing spelling games. Although Sister Marie-Louise herself did not know a word of Burmese, I somehow was perfectly able to understand what she wanted me to do. During the daytime she never made a favourite of me, but her secret kindness and encouragement meant a great deal and my standing with Sister Seraphina improved slightly, although I never lost my fear of her. What prompted Sister Marie-Louise to come to my aid was never discussed but I think Sister Seraphina from that time realised that I was not totally friendless and that she would have to answer to Sister Marie-Louise for the bruises and marks found on me. The beatings did not stop, but the intervals between them were longer.

I don't know what possessed me to do what I did one day, but as she had a hand raised to give me yet another blow I was suddenly emboldened to say, 'Sister, I want to become a Catholic.' The effect was miraculous, as her hand fell to her side and, taking me by the hand, she gave thanks to God. Relieved as I was, I had to admit to a guilty feeling, for I had received no spiritual revelation, I just wanted to stop being beaten.

While still in Sister Seraphina's class I received letters from my father who was now in the most northerly part of Burma in a place called Myitkyina, a long distance north of Mandalay, Pagan and Bhamo. Every school child in Burma is taught that the Irrawaddy is navigable right up to Bhamo where there is a famous defile. Even the Italian nuns taught us Burmese geography. My father's letters, written in English, were still too difficult for me to understand, so a senior girl was assigned to translate them into Burmese for me. In one of them he asked what I wanted for my birthday. I was still not quite sure what a birthday was, for we didn't seem to observe them in my mother's family, and even less sure what to ask for as a present, but the senior girl and her chums decided I should ask for a scooter, because they wanted one. When it eventually arrived it was so popular that I hardly had a chance to ride on it.

One day my father proposed to pay me a visit and take me away for a few days. My mother's visit had upset the administration; my father's impending arrival created panic of a different sort, although *he* would be allowed to take me away, even during the term. What alarmed the nuns was that because of spending all the holidays with my mother, I still knew very little English. So for what seemed like weeks beforehand I was drilled in conversational English to impress him. Phrases such as 'How are you Daddy?', 'I hope you had a pleasant journey', 'I can speak English very well', and 'Would you like me to read to you?' were repeated over and over again until I had mastered them.

My father arrived. I had not seen him for two years and would have been seven years old. It was strange seeing him, this tall figure, wearing khaki shorts and knee socks. He had always looked stern, as I remembered, and, though I was not exactly afraid of him, I was certainly quite shy and not very much at ease. Polite and respectful, but stiff with the effort of trying to remember all that the nuns wanted me to say, I was tongue-tied. My father looked disappointed, the Reverend Mother mortified, and to add to her mortification I broke into Burmese!

Eventually we were on our own and on the way to Taunggyi, the capital of the Southern Shan States, forty-four miles east of

Kalaw. The road was first through dense pine forest which gradually thinned out the further we went. It was extremely narrow and twisty in places where the land fell away precipitously. Lorries overloaded with goods and people clinging to the sides looked in great danger of falling over the edge, and on a couple of occasions we barely avoided colliding with bullock-carts. But my father, an experienced driver on all types of roads, seemed to be prepared for any exigencies. Luckily he had to concentrate on driving, for I was still tongue-tied and certainly no credit to the nuns. But I was so excited to be close to my father at last, and can still picture the golden hairs on his knees and down his bare forearm next to me as he controlled the juddering gear lever round those terrifying bends.

I was relieved when we stopped en route to spend a few hours with friends of his, a Mr Wright and his gentle Shan wife who tried to get me to make friends with their enormous dog called Caesar while Mr Wright and my father discussed business.

In Taunggyi we stayed at the Residency with the imposing hill known as The Crag rising behind it. I remember my father arranging for a bath to be prepared for me in an outhouse bathroom, then leaving me to attend a reception, saying he would come back for me soon. I sat in the zinc bath-tub playing with soap bubbles, but after a while the water became colder and colder and I began to think he had forgotten me. I wondered what I should do if indeed he had. At long last he turned up with an enormous towel in which he enveloped me, restoring my circulation, for by now I was shivering and covered in goose pimples.

My father and I paid a few visits to Taunggyi over the next year or so and it was here that I first met Mr Roy Ogden and

and his family. He, like my father, was in the Burma Frontier Service, serving in the Wa States on the Chinese border and had come out with my father in 1927. The most impressive thing about Mr Ogden was his height, for he must have been at least six foot six tall. With this went distinguished good looks, a remarkably soft speaking voice and gentle eyes. I also remember his large, well-shaped hands which had a special quality about them as if they could alleviate suffering.

An assistant superintendent's life could be a lonely one and also dangerous, often spent in far-flung villages where it was not possible to take a wife and family. Mrs Ogden was the daughter of a judge who had married an Anglo-Burmese woman. When I visited her recently, she recalled that in thirteen years of marriage in Burma only a total of two years were spent with her husband. When I first met her in Taunggyi I thought she was one of the most beautiful people I had ever seen. Extremely feminine and petite with the daintiest of hands and feet and dark lustrous almond eyes, she was so different from her husband who loomed over her with his enormous height. I thought her smile was as lovely as an angel's and her gentle manners soon won me over. They had a little girl, Elizabeth, about my age, and a smaller boy, Christopher. Elizabeth's birthday party was in progress when we arrived, a very happy occasion. Elizabeth later attended the convent in Kalaw as a day girl, wearing enormous bows in her hair, and the briefest of gymslips revealing the frilliest of knickers when she arrived each day with her *ayah*. The nuns shook their heads in grave disapproval at the immodesty of her dress, but could not prevail on her mother to lengthen it.

While with my father no mention was made of my mother, and it did not occur to me to ask why they were not together. It was so good to be taken out of school and bought whatever I wanted in the way of toys. I remember there was a craze for minute cups and saucers in porcelain, and patiently my father searched for them in the whole of Kalaw, finally finding them in a large department store. Knowing that I should really have been in school no doubt also contributed greatly to my enjoyment. My father could have taken me out of school as often as he wished, and the nuns would not have objected, not just because he was paying the fees, but because it was obvious they had a high regard for him, tinged with a certain amount of awe.

CHAPTER

|米|米| 5 |米|米|

SOMETHING DISASTROUS

The pattern of school and holidays continued, with me making a little progress at lessons, then going joyfully home to my mother's village which undid all I had learnt during the term. It *was* somewhat confusing to lead two such different lives: the carefree blissful family life in Sat-thwa within its gentle Buddhist framework, and in sharp contrast the over-disciplined and sometimes terrifying convent life in Kalaw. For, despite all its modern comforts, I could not help but regard it sometimes as a jungle fraught with danger, Sister Seraphina undoubtedly being the biggest hazard. Now I was in the first standard more time at school seemed to be involved with the practice of religion – and a foreign one at that. Whether one was a Hindu, Parsee, Sikh, Buddhist, Moslem or Christian, attendance at Mass was obligatory every day, and so was learning the catechism, bible-reading and mastering the other devotions such as benedictions, novenas, requiems and the Rosary. The hymns were enjoyable, however, even in Latin, and on saints' days there were processions when we all wore white dresses and veils which drew admiring glances from passers-by.

But it was a shock to find that the religious instruction given in such large doses at school dwelt so long on Heaven and Hell, more specifically the damnation to Hell of all non-Catholics, and the obligatory prayers for their conversion before this fate overtook them. It was not long before the school bullies, mostly European children, goaded me into admitting that my mother, being brown and Buddhist, would go to Hell. Fiercely protective of her, I never failed to take the bait, and their derision only served to make me hit out in a blind rage. So once more I would be led away by the supervising nun, hands tied behind my back, to be locked up in a classroom or dormitory.

There was definitely a desire among some of the Burmese to be like the British in appearance and manners. After all, were not the ruling races British and Europeans? In her village my mother had accepted a sort of star status as her due for marrying a British man. But not everyone thought of such a marriage as an honour. Some, like the headteacher in Sat-thwa, even despised her for marrying a foreigner, and every time this woman saw us her hard eyes raked us with positive dislike. The club in Kalaw was not open to Burmese or Indians, no matter how well connected or educated they were. Prejudices and bigotry were rife and complicated. People of mixed race were looked down on by both Europeans and natives and preferred to be called Anglo-Indians or Anglo-Burmans rather than Eurasian. Even the nuns were not totally free of such ingrained colour prejudice, exhorting us not to go out in the hot sun without our topees, otherwise we would become as brown as the natives!

We were afforded glimpses of the world outside the convent gates on formal walks in the evenings, crocodile-fashion, with a nun at either end. When we walked past the English Club a low whisper ordering us all to avert our gaze was passed along the line. Years later I recounted this to the Ogdens who roared with laughter at the notion that the nuns seemed to think the Club was a den of iniquity.

On Thursdays the walks were more enjoyable, often by the fast flowing stream where people and dogs swam. Along the edge of the stream grew enormous raspberry bushes with luscious berries glistening yellow in the sun and incredibly sweet to eat. There were also wild gooseberries, much bigger than the English varieties, which we would take back to school to soak in salt water to eat a week later. In the rainy season we had to contend with gleaming black leeches which not only crawled up our legs, but dropped unnoticed from dripping trees and penetrated every part of the body. The only way we could prise them off was with salt. We looked forward to one particular walk which took us high above the railway station and past a house built on a jutting rock which had enormous green iron gates with the engraving of a large fish on them. We were given to understand that a very eccentric Englishman lived there called Mr Noel Whiting who was rather frightening and that we should pass along in silence. Did we know a whiting was a fish? Probably not. Maybe we would have been less frightened of him if we had realised he could joke about his name.

Some of us did not go home every holiday, perhaps because parents were on tour, and for us a lot of events were planned. The most exciting were the day-long picnics, travelling in the brown school bus. Ahead of us went the servants bearing huge baskets containing all the food, drink, tablecloths and paraphernalia needed for the day. There would be about thirty of us at the most, and we had plenty of freedom to roam about until called to eat. We were sometimes taken to orange groves belonging to a local family, and at other times allowed to play in the enormous compounds of families who were friendly with the nuns. The reservoir some distance from the convent was also a place we frequently visited. On one occasion we were taken to the Pindaya Caves, a place of pilgrimage for devout Bhuddists, but I remember it for quite another reason. We were suddenly ordered to keep very quiet and to remain so for what seemed a very long time – a tiger was prowling just above the cave overhang.

It was now 1941 and I was eight years old. I had not gained the academic level necessary to pass into the second standard, having failed miserably in all the exams. But because I was considered too stupid to benefit any further from Sister Seraphina's teaching and still wore the stigma of a dunce, I was moved up with the rest of the class anyway.

Miss Boroni, the new teacher, was everything Sister Seraphina was not. Young, Anglo-Indian, pretty and cheerful, she wore lovely frocks with puffed sleeves and strappy wedge-heeled sandals, and her classroom seemed like a bright garden filled with the colour of beautiful flowers and bees humming and buzzing with activity – in stark contrast to Sister Seraphina's which resembled so much a gloomy and frightening prison. I can almost see Miss Boroni now, flitting from pupil to pupil making sure each and every one understood one part of a lesson before moving on to the next. When she bent over me I could catch the scent of a flowery fragrance and her frocks always had a fresh crispness. If my reputation for being a dunce had gone before me, she never showed she knew this, for she had a marvellous way of helping a child to understand what was being taught. Under her gentle and patient teaching I thrived as never before and waited eagerly for what the next day's classes would bring. The classroom was a hive of happy activity with spelling bees, oral mental arithmetic and children encouraged to express opinions both in English and Burmese.

We now had an examination once a term in religious matters, presided over by Mother Josephine, the Reverend Mother, the very same who had greeted my parents on our first arrival at the school. With her came Sister Erminia who asked the questions, Mother Josephine sitting back slightly mouthing the answers and giving us all many a prompt, while Sister Erminia pretended to be cross. Because she was so pleased with us Miss Boroni wangled special permission from the nuns to take us for the afternoon to the orange groves at Loi-an (the owners were friends of hers) where we were free to roam among the rows and rows of trees, before enjoying a marvellous tea. Compared with what had gone before, the year was one of unbelievable happiness and achievement and at the end-of-year results I found that I came third in a class of twenty, not far behind an extremely clever girl called Vera Tai, a daughter of the Sawbwa of Kentung, whose older sister was the head girl. All the same, at the concert which marked the end of the school year I was given the part of Dopey in *Snow White and the Seven Dwarfs*. Made up with a snowy white beard and hat and an enormous puffy jacket exquisitely finished by the school's Indian tailor, I felt I looked the part and was caught up in the thrill of the performance. It was wonderful to hear the encouraging applause as we were called on to do an encore of the dwarfs coming home from work, even if neither of my parents was in the indulgent audience.

The Christmas holidays came and with them the cool season. Already the rest of the children had gone home and I felt sure that it would not be long before my mother came for me. Yet day passed after day and still she did not arrive, and no explanation was given to me. Now I was the only one left in school, with no one but the servants for company. Old Joseph, Father Boldrini's Tamil man-servant, was one of my favourites. Three times a day he crossed the road from the church to the convent to collect Father Boldrini's food in a tiffin-carrier. He had a beautiful daughter, Josephine, who must have been about seventeen and I loved to stay by her as she washed the clothes outside her kitchen door. Occasionally I was allowed to help them polish the enormous candlesticks used in the church and also the very tall brass vases placed on the altar with the beautiful wild arum lilies which grew so profusely in the nearby valley.

Sometimes also Mother Josephine would ask me to help her thread her needle as she sewed in the nuns' quiet period. It was at times like these that she would tell me how I embarrassed them by telling my father we were not given enough soap, and she would remind me of all the times that my mother brought me back to school late. But she smiled as she recounted these things, so was not cross. Sometimes I thought that she was on the point of telling me something important but she always seemed to to hold back. I was sure that the servants also were whispering about me, for they would stop as soon as they were aware that I was in their midst. One day I was summoned to be measured for new clothes by the Indian tailor. The materials were quite strange to me for they were warm and heavy, but the dresses were very pretty with puffed up sleeves just like Miss Boroni's. My mysterious new clothes reminded me of the nuns' custom of changing their habits from white in the hot season to black in the cool season, for Kalaw could be quite cold in the early mornings and evenings. Trying not to show it, they looked slightly self-conscious as they adjusted the tucks and gathers and fussed over the fall of the voluminous skirts not worn since the previous season.

Two or three times a week I was escorted by the *mali* to spend the day with the local magistrate and his wife. Mr and Mrs Poulton were childless and Mrs Poulton always made a big fuss over me. Mr Poulton, extremely stout and red of face, would play games where he would spring out on me from a hiding place, booming in a terrible voice and really terrifying me. Sometimes I was taken to spend the day with Mrs Ogden who was now living in Kalaw and this was a special treat. Very much later she told me how frightened I was most of the time, clinging to her skirts and seldom venturing from her presence.

Christmas was near, the first I was ever aware of, for my mother in her village never celebrated Christmas and had not heard of it. I knew roughly what it signified and that because it was Christmas I would be receiving presents from the Poultons and the nuns. For all that, I was rather lonely and could not shake off a premonition of impending disaster. Nothing could be learned from the servants – they were not to be coaxed into letting me know what they knew, but I did not have long to wait. On Christmas Eve 1941 the Japanese bombed Rangoon.

That something disastrous had happened I was aware, but I was totally ignorant of the real state of things. Days went by, and still no one came to take me away for the holidays. I grew uneasy and did not know what to think. There were no letters from my father and my mother had not sent word to explain why she did not come for me. Left to my own devices I roamed all over the convent (except for the part called the community quarters belonging to the nuns). Sometimes I loitered near the boundary of the compound, often seeing a very pretty English girl on horseback, rather older than me. Once I plucked up enough courage to say hello to her, and she told me that her name was Gemma, the niece of a Mrs Childers who lived near the convent and was a good friend of the nuns. I thought Gemma was the epitome of Englishness, with perfect poise, looking so elegant on her horse, and I was happy to worship her from a distance.

On another occasion I was called to meet a girl of my own age called Sylvia Hockey whose parents had just arrived in Kalaw and who were thinking of placing her in the convent. From the start we got on very well and I was quite often allowed to spend the day with her.

When the school term started again in January, only a small proportion of the children came back, and a very different atmosphere prevailed, as though it was understood that life and lessons were now proceeding on a makeshift basis. It was nevertheless exciting for, now promoted to the third standard, I was looking forward to writing with a fountain pen, one that my father had given me on his previous visit.

The lack of any sense of permanence persisted, for soon a lot of the children were being taken away again by their parents. There was excitement in the air and rumours flew of an invasion by the Japanese. Truckloads of British soldiers in khaki suddenly appeared on the roads, and quite often jeeps rolled up with army officers who came to talk to the nuns. Soon there were only eight children left, including Lucy and Mary Grey, sent up from the sister convent in Toungoo a hundred miles north of Rangoon which had been badly bombed by the Japanese; two beautiful flaxen-haired German girls called Herta and Eva Webb, Monique Rowland, Sylvia Hockey and myself. The Webb children with hair of spun gold worn in plaits, eyes of translucent blue and delicate skin, faintly rose-tinted, drew me like a magnet. They must have been just like the children of ancient Britain who caught St Augustine's attention and made him exclaim, 'Angels, not Angles!' Eva the younger, plump and languid, was surely born to sit on silk cushions and be fed strawberries and cream. But Herta with her flashing mischievous eyes and sense of fun would always be the leader of the gang.

The nuns were gravely preoccupied with world affairs and quite unable to superintend us to the former extent. So while we waited one evening after baths for the usual hair and fingernails inspection before night prayers, we found ourselves in the unusual position of being unsupervised.

'Let's play Ring a Ring of Roses,' suggested Herta with just a suspicion of an order in her voice. Obediently we formed ourselves into a ring holding hands and we skipped first one way around the room, and then the other.

'Now,' ordered Herta, 'lift your nighties up or drop your pyjamas!'

There was no need for her to add, 'I dare you!' It was there in her voice and in the glint in her eye, and we were too taken aback to refuse. As we hesitated she pulled off her pyjamas and kicked them aside saying, 'Go on, are you scared? Who's scared?'

Goaded by her taunts and chivvied by her pointing finger we hastened to obey, looking at each other sheepishly the while and feeling acutely uncomfortable. I wished the earth would open up and swallow me but just as I began to wonder what was coming next, footsteps could be heard in the passage and we scurried to our bedsides. When the nun came in it was to find us all ready for night prayers kneeling by our beds, the dormitory a picture of order without any hint of the mischief we had been up to only a few minutes before.

On the war front, a sense of urgency was injected into our situation when the townspeople began coming up to the convent in droves bearing their valuables and begging the nuns to look after them before they took flight. None of them thought it would be long before they would be able to return and reclaim their property. The Kalaw Hotel deposited huge wooden trunks containing linen and silver, and the Poultons left a beautifully carved camphor chest for safe-keeping. There were fond farewells and a flurry of handkerchiefs as the departing townspeople waved good-bye.

Soon after, the convent was swarming with British soldiers, and we were loaded into trucks together with all our beds, desks, tables, pianos and statues. The army needed our convent and moved us to a house a couple of miles away called Salween. It was a large house without a doubt, but still too small for all the nuns, children and servants, and we were terribly squashed. Because of the chaos and cramped conditions lessons took place outside, but concentration was difficult for we were all aware of an undercurrent of excitement. Oddly enough it was here that I learnt two poems which gripped my imagination – 'The Sands of Dee' ('Oh Mary, go and call the cattle home') by Charles Kingsley, and Wordsworth's 'Lucy Gray'. I would go in search of floating weeds in the well, as in the first poem, or peer under rocks, hoping to catch a glimpse of a violet, as in 'Lucy Gray'. For Salween had beautiful fairytale grounds and there was ample opportunity to explore and enjoy them. The pine trees swayed in the breeze making a soft soothing sound, depositing a fine film of green dust over the furniture. The *mali* taught us how to erect wigwams of bamboo and pine needles. At night he patrolled the grounds, bearing an enormous well-sharpened *dah*.

Just as suddenly as we had arrived at Salween, we departed, herded once more into army trucks by the British soldiers, and taken back to the convent. They were leaving altogether, and that as fast as they could. No sooner had we been unceremoniously dumped than the trucks crammed with soldiers began moving out at high speed. Some soldiers in danger of being left behind had to run after them to catch up, their comrades leaning over the tailgate to give them a helping hand.

While still at Salween, our numbers had dwindled to three – Lucy and Mary Grey and myself. In less than a week, early in 1942, the Japanese marched into the convent.

CHAPTER
|✳|✳| 6 |✳|✳|

ENTER THE JAPANESE

ONE OF THE FIRST things the nuns did on our return to the convent was to lay a hurried plan for our safety in case we were invaded or bombed by the Japanese, for by now their low-flying planes were dropping leaflets in English informing us that we would soon be liberated from the 'imperialist' British. The large red rising sun blazed down on us from the underside of the aeroplane wings, threatening us with their display of confident strength. The safest place for us all, the nuns decided, was the space beneath the large chapel where it was possible to stand upright to a good distance from the door. No light whatsoever penetrated the space, it could not be reached through the floor of the chapel but only through a door built into the stonework. All in all it seemed the soundest idea in case of a bomb attack.

We children knew that we were supposed to be afraid, and we acted the part in the presence of the nuns, but truth to tell it was all so very exciting that it was difficult to keep up the pretence when on our own. Luckily, very little notice was taken of us, and while the servants put about the rumours they heard, we sat and listened, and for the first time felt well informed. So we vied with each other to see who would spy the Japanese first, knowing it would not be long now before they appeared. And we were right. Even at a distance we could hear their marching feet tramping up the road in front of the convent, the very road down which my parents had driven when I saw them together for the last time four years before.

Soon we caught our first sight of the conquerors, a long line of soldiers, three or four abreast, clad in khaki, flaps hanging from their caps, bayonets glinting in the sun. It was a compelling sight and we were unable to tear ourselves away, until the nuns seeing them as well, half pushed, half dragged us to the underground space. Mother Superior and Sister Erminia, having made sure we were all safely locked up, hurried up to the chapel itself and barricaded themselves in the sacristy above. In an uncharacteristic display of fear and panic the nuns sent up loud prayers for our deliverance which must have been heard by anyone outside the wall. Soon the soldiers could be heard marching up the gravel drive to the accompaniment of loud guttural orders. The noise their hob-nailed boots made next told us they were racing up the stone steps into the chapel and the sacristy itself. In no time our door was battered in and before our terrified gaze Mother Superior and Sister Erminia were pushed at bayonet-point into our midst. Now we were really scared – there was no pretence, for behind the bayonets were round yellow faces with narrow slit eyes full of menace and hate, snapping orders we didn't understand. The same bayonets pushed us out into the sunshine and we were surrounded.

An officer speaking English asked Mother Superior, 'You English?' It took some time to establish that most of our community were Italian. Relaxing a little, for the Italians were their allies, but still keeping us in a group, the soldiers ordered a search of the entire convent. The nuns protested at the outrage to the chapel but gave way before the menacing bayonets. Satisfied that we were not harbouring any British or Chinese and leaving sentries at the gates, the soldiers formed up and marched away, having given us to understand that we were all to report to the Kalaw Hotel the next day.

Thoroughly frightened yet excited by the day's events, we wondered what would happen next. While the senior nuns discussed our situation, the junior ones tried to go about their duties as best they could, until Mother Superior and Sister Erminia were ready to give us our instructions for the next day. They sought to impress on us the gravity of the situation and the need for prayer. They also tried to reassure us by saying that the Japanese would not harm us or take us away, *provided* we three children with our British connections kept perfect silence and did nothing that would draw attention to us. We were to let the nuns do the talking.

In orderly fashion the next day, the ten nuns, two servants and the three of us set out for the Kalaw Hotel. Already gathered in the compound were other residents of Kalaw. Amongst them we recognised some day pupils, the school doctor Major Hamilton, some Anglo-Indian teachers, Father Boldrini with Joseph and Josephine, many other Anglo-Indians and Anglo-Burmese, the rich Persian shop-owners, such as the Shirazees and their numerous families, but hardly any Burmese. A space had been cleared for a table at which sat three Japanese soldiers, with some non-Japanese interpreters. Soldiers stood at intervals with bayonets. A low murmur ran through the crowd which stopped abruptly whenever orders were given by the soldiers.

It was a fiery hot day and the sun scorched down on us, making rivulets of perspiration run down our necks. For a long time nothing seemed to happen but, remembering the dire warnings given by Mother Superior, we tried very hard not to fidget or grumble. Suddenly proceedings got under way. One by one people were roughly escorted to the table, ordered to bow very low and the interrogation began. It was not easy to find out what was going on, but the questioning was done in a very harsh and guttural tone which alone was frightening. If answers were not forthcoming or were unsatisfactory a blow to the side of the head with a rifle butt produced results. Sometimes a group of people would be marched off. Would we ever see them again?

It was now our turn, Mother Superior at the head and the three of us, closely guarded by Sister Erminia, last. The Japanese interrogating officer spoke perfect, if stilted English, wanting to know where our parents were, clearly believing that they must be close by. Sister Erminia explained that the Greys had been sent up from their Toungoo convent which had been badly bombed, that all their papers had been destroyed and that they had not seen their father for a very long time. As for me my father was Irish, not English. This explanation seemed to satisfy the officer and, after relaying this to his superior, we were allowed to go; but not before each of us was issued with a badge denoting our nationality in Japanese characters which we were to have pinned on us at all times. Ordering all of us to bow very low every time we saw a Japanese, we were dismissed.

On the walk back to the convent everyone was quiet. Things had gone better than we had feared and we had escaped lightly, but we had seen enough of the methods of interrogation by the Japanese to convince ourselves that now we were an occupied country. Seeing harmless, innocent people being hit on the head with rifle butts was a terrifying and sobering lesson and we knew that there would now be a great deal of change. It must have required an enormous amount of courage for Sister Erminia to respond to the interrogation in that calm, dignified way of hers, and we were greatly impressed and filled with a silent gratitude, for we had seen some of the other children in that gathering not so lightly treated.

Thus sobered, we embarked on a completely new way of life. We knew we would have to stifle anxieties about the unknown plight of our parents for the time being. It was almost as though we had in that short space, acquired a wisdom beyond our years, and we were determined not to add to the problems now faced by the nuns.

In the short week between our return to the convent and the arrival of the Japanese a few sudden exchanges of nuns had been made. Our Mother Superior, Mother Josephine, the dreaded Sister Seraphina and Sister Amalia went elsewhere, perhaps to the convent in Taunggyi, and the new Mother Superior was now Mother Irma, younger than Mother Josephine and an unknown quantity. There were still fifteen of us, ten nuns, mostly Italian, one Karen servant called Teresina or Tracy who must have had the sharpest knuckles in the world, and one Tamil servant who went by the strange name of Aridiem Mary, perhaps to avoid confusion with Mary Grey. One of the Gurkha *mali*s chose to stay with us with his large family, and there was a terrified Chinese carpenter called John (the name given to all Chinese carpenters). The Chinese suffered terribly at the hands of the Japanese and, although we did all we could to allay his fears, hiding him at the first glimpse of a Japanese, he could not control his quaking at the very mention of them. But our efforts were in vain – word had got about that he was hiding in our midst and he was most brutally dragged away, never to be seen again. Professing ignorance of his presence with all their might, the nuns nevertheless received dire warnings lest they even think about repeating such a foolhardy act.

The convent was vast, spreading itself out on three levels and Mother Superior decided that we should all now live in two main buildings. All but a couple of nuns remained in the original house, and the rest of us occupied what used to be the boys' dormitory on top, and the kindergarten below. The *mali* and his family stayed in the original quarters housing outdoor servants. There was also a fierce dog called Bobby who hated the Japanese and could only be controlled by Sister Marie-Louise, and a more friendly rough-haired terrier called Fido. Our lives were completely different now. Lessons were dispensed with because it was strictly forbidden to teach English, but as most of the nuns could not communicate with us in any other language, English was allowed in conversation.

Instead of lessons we had jobs. No longer having electricity or running water, we depended on hurricane lamps and water brought in every day by the *mali* in large kerosene oil cans. The job of cleaning the lamps and trimming the wicks was left to us and I loved it. Everything about a hurricane lamp works so smoothly. The glass globe, so well secured in its wire harness, tilts obligingly so that the glass can be released for cleaning. This had to be done carefully, for replacements could not be had. We then raised the wick and trimmed it if necessary, filled the well with kerosene oil, and put the whole lamp together again. Today

I still find it hard to resist stepping in when passing a chandler's shop just to touch one of these lamps and transport myself back to such a different world. Sweeping the verandahs, a job previously done by an Indian *jarruwallah*, and keeping the compound clear of litter were other of our chores, along with cleaning the brass candlesticks and vases used in the chapel.

But there was still time for games. The games we played at the convent were very different from those I had played with mud and water and bits of broken crockery in Sat-thwa. Now there were exciting team games such as *aung thu* (winners) which required as many people as possible, and which we loved to play by the light of the moon on a pitch similar to that used for netball. The defending team manned the lines and the attackers had to break through without being touched, and get back to the starting point. It called for ingenuity to distract the opposition and agility to weave and dive through the defence. Aridiem Mary could always be cajoled into taking part as she was very fleet of foot. Teresina usually refused as she was flat-footed, a handicap we took advantage of to escape her clouts which she dispensed as liberally as Father Boldrini dispensed indulgences during Lent and All Souls.

A game which required great concentration was called *gillie dunda*. Indian in origin, it required a bat and a small piece of wood like a cricket bail. The player struck the bail at one of the pointed ends and tried to hit it away as far as possible, the distance being measured with the bat. Whoever hit it furthest was the winner.

We also played the British game of five or seven stones which involves throwing one stone in the air while retrieving the ones on the ground in sequence before catching the first stone. If we were lucky enough to find a marble it became almost a leisurely game, as it gave us more time to pick up the other stones while the marble was allowed to bounce once. So our days were filled with activity at the convent, but there was always in the background the knowledge that at any moment everything could change at the whim of the occupying power. We learnt to look over our shoulders.

CHAPTER

|❋|❋| 7 |❋|❋|

UNDER THE RISING SUN

It was almost dusk one evening and Lucy, Mary and I were playing a last game of General Post, chasing each other round the solid wooden pillars of the portico under the teachers' dormitory when we were startled by the ghostly appearance of a tall woman in European dress gliding in out of the shadows. She was in a pathetic state, her clothing torn and filthy, her face too blood-stained and bruised to allow her to speak, but I recognised her almost at once as Mrs Childers, the aunt of Gemma with whom I had struck up an acquaintance in those lonely Christmas holidays. As I whispered her name, she put her hand cautiously to her lips and then fell senseless to the ground. We ran to get the nuns and they carried her gently up the stairs to what had been the teachers' quarters. With great kindness they nursed her back to health, for they possessed excellent nursing skills, taking all her meals to her room and keeping a watchful eye out for any sign of the Japs, as we now called them. She never came out until after dark, sometimes watching us play by the light of the hurricane lamps, now and again managing a faint smile, but not much more.

We learned from Teresina that Mrs Childers and Gemma had made their way to Myitkyina right up in the north and got on the last flight leaving Burma before the Japanese invasion. But the plane had been shot down, killing Gemma. Stricken with grief, her aunt had decided against attempting the perilous border crossing on foot and had somehow made her way all the way back to Kalaw. Often she travelled through dense jungle so as to avoid villages for fear of bumping into the Japs, sometimes she met helpful villagers, others drove her away for fear of retaliation. Miraculously, she evaded the enemy, and, so full of admiration were the nuns for this brave lady, that they were prepared to risk a great deal to keep her safe.

Mrs Childers also brought news of another passenger who had survived that last fatal flight, Lucy and Mary's father, Wilfred Grey. An employee of Steel Brothers in Rangoon, after the first bombing of the city he had been assigned the task of getting the company wives and children on planes that would take them to safety in India. He had instructed the nuns to take his daughters to the airstrip at Heho, twenty-two miles east of Kalaw, every day, because it was here that the Steel Brothers wives and children congregated in the hope of getting on a flight to Myitkyina and thence to India. With the coming and going of the other children, and the excitement of seeing so many soldiers all over the place with their trucks and jeeps, I had not noticed the daily absences of Lucy and Mary. I don't know how the nuns managed to follow Mr Grey's instructions, what with the scarcity of civilian transport and the time involved, but they did so faithfully, waiting each day for him to collect the girls and returning them disappointed to the convent each evening, only to repeat the attempt the next day. But it gradually became obvious that something had happened to prevent him carrying out his intentions, and with heavy hearts the children accepted that the conclusion the nuns came to was right – there was no further point in waiting in Heho.

Mrs Childers now reported that the last time she saw their father he was alive and well, having survived the crash, but that he had decided it was his duty to look after the other survivors, the wives and children trying to make the rest of their way on foot through terrible jungle territory to safety in India. Lucy and Mary received this news quietly. They never seemed to want to talk to others about it, communing with each other in a secret language and exchanging meaningful looks from which I felt excluded.

When they arrived in Kalaw after the bombing of Toungoo they had become separated from their papers, so it was not known how old they were. The nuns solved this by making Lucy a year older and Mary a year younger than me. They were already Catholics and must have been converted when very young at their Toungoo convent. Mrs Grey had come from a wealthy Burmese sawmill-owning family and had been a teacher before her marriage. She died giving birth to a little boy who also did not survive. This was when Mr Grey sent the girls off to the convent with strict instructions to the nuns that their Burmese relations were not to be allowed to see them. They also had a little brother called John who had had to be left behind with friends in Rangoon because of a broken leg.

Though Lucy and Mary must have been bitterly disappointed at never meeting up with their father at Heho, I envied them the companionship they had in each other and I yearned for a sister of my own. For my part I knew nothing of my own family's fate, having had no news of my parents since before that mysterious Christmas holiday when no one came to take me away, and when I was being measured for those curious warm clothes. But we were brought up in a way which must seem extremely unnatural to a child of today. Blind obedience was expected and exacted from us, to the point of not asking questions, even when we were dying to know the why, what, when and how of our circumstances. To put questions to the nuns about this would imply gross ingratitude on our part, for it would be taken as doubting that the nuns had our whole good uppermost in their minds. We therefore had to stifle as best we could our deep anxiety for our parents and the insecurity that would creep up on us. We compensated by always trying to eavesdrop on the servants. Eavesdropping on the nuns did no good, for their conversation was mostly in Italian.

We were left unmolested at the convent for most of the time, but every so often the Japanese soldiers would swoop down on us to make a random check, remembering that we had once harboured a Chinese. On these occasions the nuns hid Mrs Childers in places unknown to us. Knowing that we were never to give the game away, it was disconcerting to find a soldier so suddenly in our midst, and we often wondered if the Japanese had their suspicions.

One day not long after the arrival of Mrs Childers we received orders that everyone in the convent was to learn Japanese, a soldier being assigned to us for this task. No one was excused, from the eldest nun in her seventies down to Lucy, Mary and me. The lessons took place daily in what had been the kindergarten. The nuns made very poor pupils, while we three children made rapid progress, often having to help them with their homework, and what a very novel experience we found that to be. Failure to produce good work brought severe punishment from the soldier, and caning was threatened. One of the first things we learnt, even before the alphabet or numbers, was the 'Kimigayo', the national anthem. Poor Sister Antonietta, our new music teacher, had to try and play it by ear on the piano and found this very difficult as it was so very different from any style of music to which she was accustomed. The words meant nothing to us, the music seemed very alien and the nuns could not get to grips with the unusual timing or beat. Yet we had to sing it every day, standing rigidly to attention, for if there was so much as a fidget or wobble, down would come the cane on the backs of our legs. Not even the nuns were spared the daily ordeal. As a result I can remember the Japanese words to this day, but it was only recently I was provided with an English translation, and very quaint it proves to be. It makes five short lines in Japanese which are sung twice. The English rendering by B.H. Chamberlain runs as follows:

> Ten thousand years of happy reign be thine:
> Rule on, my lord, till what are pebbles now
> By ages united to mighty rocks shall grow
> Whose venerable sides the moss doth line.

The ancient Japanese poet addressing his Emperor certainly had a very hazy notion of geology.

The classes did not continue for more than about three months after which our Japanese soldier-teacher seemed to give up the unequal struggle. Once the nuns were certain that he would not come again they began to think of ways of giving us

[69]

some sort of an education. Because it was well known that the Japanese were great lovers of music, flowers and children, the idea occurred to them that they might manage to teach us some English under the guise of music lessons, which were permitted. Considerable vigilance was still needed, however, both in keeping Mrs Childers safe and continuing our English, for it would not do to be found engaged in either activity. By now no writing books or pencils were available but slates and slate pencils were, so these were brought out and used constantly, with the advantage that the evidence could be wiped away if we had an unexpected Japanese visit.

Sister Erminia took us for religious instruction. Instead of the boring and mechanical questions and answers of the catechism, she delved into the beautiful stories of the Old Testament, holding us enthralled. She also taught us geography making that subject another great favourite. Sister Christine, who was part Goan, part British, was our English teacher and she struggled valiantly to get us to love the fiendishly incomprehensible mysteries of parsing and analysing as much as she did. Maths was shared by Sister Erminia and Sister Christine. Sister Anita took us for needlework – an expert at it herself, she had a losing battle from the start, for we detested it so much that we did all we could to make ourselves unavailable on some pretext or other. Sister Antonietta gave us music lessons and here I had a head start, for during those Christmas holidays when I had been on my own Mother Josephine had thought it would be a good idea for Sister Amalia to give me some music lessons. It had been a slow beginning and I had been allowed to practise on the piano in the parlour so that she could be within earshot to make sure that I was really practising tedious five-finger exercises and not picking out tunes and wasting time.

There had also been distractions which I enjoyed, watching parents coming and going in cars to collect their offspring. I remember a boy called Eugene Lightbody with bright carroty red hair and masses of freckles, especially on his nose, with a very jolly mother who had asked Sister Amalia what I was doing in school all on my own, then rattled on, not giving her a chance to reply. This was most disappointing for I had been straining to hear her explanation. All that seemed a world away now, but at least I knew my way around the keyboard.

We were still paid random visits by the soldiers, and it was on one of these that Mrs Childers was discovered. How, we never found out. Perhaps we had been watched as we played in the dusk when she was wont to come down and silently enjoy watching us. There was no warning. Four soldiers burst in among us one afternoon and without any hesitation marched their way to her room at the top of the stairs. Another soldier stood at the bottom barring the way up and thus we all stood helplessly below, hearing the guttural voices shouting and giving orders. They emerged some minutes later, surrounding her completely, but as she was taller than they, we saw that her head was bleeding profusely and her clothes were in disarray. We had not heard her utter so much as a cry, although she must have received quite a battering to be in such a state. Powerless to intervene, and greatly shaken ourselves, we looked on as she was led away, bayonets prodding her unnecessarily. As they passed, Mother Superior stretched out her hands in a gesture of sympathy towards Mrs Childers, hoping she would realise that we would not have betrayed her for anything in the world, but one of the soldiers butted her away with his rifle as a warning. We felt the brave lady understood, as with bloody head held high she was marched away. We never saw her again, although once or twice word got to the nuns that she was held prisoner in an unknown camp, impressing everyone with her dignity and courage, and still managing to be as fastidious in her dress and appearance as ever. Sister Christine constantly held her up as an example for us to imitate in every way and, even though we shared her admiration for Mrs Childers, we did grow weary of her repetitious nagging.

It certainly was a very different life that we children led now. Never having to lift a finger or do any kind of manual work before the invasion, once the novelty wore off we found our imposed chores very tedious and performed them with ill grace. But busy as Teresina and Aridiem Mary were in the kitchen, we were never called to help them there. It was as though an ingrained idea of our station in life made it seem improper for the three of us to be seen in the kitchen. Our meals were brought out to us in the schoolroom, although we would have been more than happy to collect them for ourselves. The nuns also had to undertake all kinds of manual labour formerly left to the Indian coolies. One day before her departure I saw the hated Sister Seraphina cleaning a lavatory with her bare hands. With shattering clarity it was brought home to me that the old life was really over. The very first sight of a white person doing a menial dirty job was a severe jolt.

CHAPTER

|✳|✳| 8 |✳|✳|

LEARNING TO ADJUST

JUST LIKE THE BRITISH, the Japanese in turn wanted the convent for their own use. They moved us to two neighbouring houses on the outskirts of a collection of bamboo-hutted villages. One was two-storeyed and the other about three hundred yards away, a bungalow called Summerville. Father Boldrini was also moved to a third house close to us, together with his retainers. The *mali* and his family, quartered in a large hut near the house, still carried on with the heavy work. The bungalow contained the dining rooms and chapel with living quarters for two or three nuns, while the rest of us were squashed into the two-storeyed house.

From all the houses we could see the three villages of bamboo huts separated by tarmac roads lined with cherry blossom trees. Between them and us stretched the paddy-fields, terraced and flooded in the rainy season. Rows of workers, bent double up to their calves in muddy water, transplanted the baby rice seedlings. All we saw of them were the broad-brimmed Shan bamboo hats called *kamauks* tied under their chins. Sometimes we saw buffaloes pulling makeshift ploughs in the shallow muddy water, driven by little boys squatting behind their heads.

The gardens of our houses and that of Father Boldrini were like paradise, stocked with fruit trees of every variety: pomelos, like big sweet pink grapefruit, guava, pears, oranges, limes, mangoes, damsons, durians, bananas and pineapple bushes. I often wondered what kind of people had lived in these houses and came to the conclusion that they must have been British, for I had never seen a Burmese garden laid out like these. Sometimes not quite ripe mangoes or damsons were shaken from the trees by the *mali* into blankets we held outstretched beneath, to be buried in sacks of rice to ripen slowly. Bananas picked green were particularly successful ripened by this method.

We still had unannounced visits from the Japanese so lessons were spasmodic, but piano lessons continued. We had progressed sufficiently to be able to tackle the simplest trios and duets, although we did not much enjoy playing together. There was always a fight about who got the most difficult or easy part or if one's hand was not removed quickly enough to make room for another hand, as the music demanded it. And we did not like the feel of each other's arms and elbows in such close proximity, so we fought our way all through the trios and duets. But Sister Christine wanted to show off her work with us and thought up concerts to be held on feast or saints' days. For these occasions she would work hard composing words in praise and gratitude to the Mother Superior to such favourite tunes of hers

as the Brahms Lullaby. We found these excruciatingly embar-
rassing as we stood in front of an audience of nuns, Mother
Superior smiling especially encouragingly, our hands rigidly to
our sides, fingers pinching each other if we thought one or the
other came in too soon or too late.

One concert must have pleased Mother Superior greatly for
she decided that we should be rewarded by being given a pet of
our own, and we were each given a duckling to rear. It is hard
to express just how happy this made us for we spent almost the
entire day looking after the little things, digging up worms in the
compound, making small ponds for them to swim in, picking
them up and setting them down as soon as we thought we had
a better place for them. Growing very fat, they could hardly
waddle about, and we put them to bed every night in the hen
house. Smiling in amusement Mother Superior watched all our
antics, suggesting we give the ducklings a bit of peace. One terrible morning we found them all dead – killed by a weasel. We
were inconsolable and moped about for days. To make up for
this loss Mother Superior got us a kid. Delighted, once again we
devoted all our effort to looking after it, dragging it from place
to place and fighting terribly over it. As we gave it no peace or
chance to graze, it did anything but thrive and, after many warnings from Mother Superior, it was finally taken away, leaving us
once more disconsolate.

We had two great dislikes – one was ironing day, usually on a
Thursday. This was the day when the nuns, having washed and
starched all their bonnets and the priest's vestments the day
before, would spend the whole day ironing them. Our duty was
to keep a regular supply of hot live coals in the brazier with
which to fill the irons. The peculiar egg-shaped apparatus used
to puff out the bonnets was also plunged into the red hot coals,

and we kept the charcoal burning by fanning or blowing through a hollow bamboo, a process which made us dizzy and faint. Candle drippings, tied up in a clean rag, were used to keep the iron surfaces clean and smooth, filling the air with a pungent smell of candle grease. Getting the bonnets to the right degree of stiffness and the ties straight and uncurled demanded a great deal of expertise, something Sister Christine did not possess. It was almost pathetic watching her trying to get to grips with it as many a bonnet was scorched, much to the annoyance of Mother Superior.

An even more hateful chore was teasing cotton from mattresses. Mattresses and mosquito nets were worth their weight in gold and had to be carefully maintained. The buttoning would first have to be removed, one top seam opened and all the cotton which had hardened into balls transferred to a pillow case, a few handfuls at a time. Then we inserted a stick with a cross-piece near one end and twirled it between our palms and as we did so the hardened balls in the pillow case would be teased out and become soft once more. The mattresses would then have to be restuffed, the buttoning placed in position and the seam resewn. Long before the task was completed our hands would become red and raw with the continuous twirling, while fluff got up our noses and into our eyes.

One night we heard a rampaging as though a vast body was hurling itself against anything in its path. The sound of crushed metal, splintering wood and pounding earth seemed to be aiming straight for us and we clung to each other wondering whether we would survive such an assault. But the destroying force seemed to give us a miss. The light of dawn revealed devastation all around. The *mali* said that a rogue elephant had been on the loose and evidence was there in the flattened water barrels, the demolition of the side walls of the verandah and the sturdy hen houses, as well as tree trunks lying across open spaces. The *mali* was kept busy for days putting things to rights and clearing up the mess.

The two houses we occupied were at the bottom of a hill, while half-way up it and few hundred yards from us was Father Boldrini's. The hill was densely wooded, and wood was very much needed as it was used for all cooking. Without any prompting from the nuns we borrowed *dahs* from the *mali*, climbed the hill, and set to cutting as much of the wood as we could, tied it into bundles, loaded it on our backs and brought it down the hill again to the kitchen. It was odd that we did so without fear of the snakes which lurked in any wooded area, for by now, having grown out of our shoes, we had to go in our bare feet, unaware of the risks we were taking. It was not entirely a wish to be helpful which prompted us to occupy ourselves in the woods – the real reason was that wild horses could not drag the nuns up that hill, and thus it was a good way of getting away from their supervision or from some other detested chores.

Someone or other was always thinking up new ways of keeping us busy and the idea came up that we should manufacture our own cloth! It was decided to experiment with the long pithy, thorny spear-like leaves of a bush similar to a pineapple. They would be soaked in tall barrels of water until the pith rotted away leaving what the nuns hoped would be long strands of fibre to make into fabric. It fell to us to check the state of the rotting vegetation, as day by day the barrels stank higher to heaven. To hasten matters we had to remove the evil-smelling mess out of the barrels and beat the remaining pulp, leaving the coarse strands to bleach in the sun. It was extremely unpleasant to handle and to our immense relief, but not soon enough, the result was considered unsatisfactory and we were allowed to give up the experiment.

A much better idea (to our way of thinking) and more restful, was to unpick socks we had outgrown to obtain cotton for sewing. Very carefully we were taught to unpick a sock at the most strategic place, a stitch at a time, until the cotton could be unravelled quite easily into balls. The nuns were skillful at sewing, keeping us all adequately and decently clad by the clever adjusting of length and width of clothes as we grew. If Sister Erminia could be cajoled into reading or telling us stories throughout the operation the tedium was greatly relieved.

With so much land available we were encouraged to dig our own little plots and experiment with growing vegetables. It was amazing how seeds of maize or beans sown in the evening would result in baby plants the next morning and we thoroughly enjoyed our gardening.

Food was plentiful if a bit boring; we grew most of it ourselves. Rice was eaten three times a day, mostly with vegetables, bamboo shoots and a variety of wild mushrooms found at the base of pine trees, looking very much like part of a coral reef and very tasty. We hardly ever had meat.

Although we had poultry, eggs were kept for the chronically ill nuns and so was milk, when available. On the whole we were quite healthy at this stage, although Lucy and Mary suffered severe bouts of malaria, no doubt brought on by having lived in a much less benign climate while they were in Toungoo. I escaped malaria, but was very often covered in sores which erupted and turned septic and painful. Toothpaste was unheard of; instead we used salt or chewed lumps of charcoal to clean our teeth and never had the benefit of a dentist for the duration of the war. One of the younger nuns suffered terribly from toothache, and after two days of hearing her scream in pain the help of a Japanese dentist was sought, bringing relief at last and putting an end to the screaming.

For a while no restrictions were placed on our movements; we could come and go as we pleased so long as we remembered to bow extremely low whenever we met a Japanese, and also to wear our badges showing our nationality. One day came the alarming news that the villages opposite were stricken by bubonic plague. Many deaths occurred, and if the funeral happened to be of someone known to the convent we had to attend it in the Catholic cemetery. Being the smallest of the crowd we were always pushed to the edge of the grave, although curiosity would anyway have drawn us like a magnet. At the first such funeral something totally unexpected took place – the lid of the coffin was unscrewed and to our horror revealed the dead face of the former school doctor, Major Hamilton. We had known him as a florid, red-faced man, but the corpse now exposed to our view was a ghastly yellow, his folded hands revealing fingernails black with dirt.

The lids of all the plague coffins were removed and, subjected to this horrible custom, we had nightmares for weeks to come. The reason for this opening of coffins was not clear to us. It was Mary's opinion that this was done to pay one's last respects to the dead. Lucy said it was to make quite sure that the person was really dead. For my part, I only wished we never had to go to another funeral as the dead faces haunted my dreams. Soon the plague became uncontrollable and the only recourse left was to burn the villages down. The picture stands out sharply in my memory, the orange fire engulfing the whole village as the bamboo huts readily went up in flames, a picture so vivid and clear-cut that it is retained in my mind's eye forever.

[79]

Having no access to a radio or newspapers, we were totally unaware of the world situation. Indeed, anyone found with a radio was shot on the spot, and now and again terrible stories reached us of Japanese atrocities, particularly against any Chinese found sheltering in the villages. Suspects were strung up between two trees tensioned with ropes, which were then split asunder, and people suspected of witholding information from the Japs had boiling water poured down their throats. We understood that we were being treated comparatively leniently because Italy was on the same side as Germany. Frequently we were gathered together when a Japanese officer appeared, immaculate in his highly polished boots, pistol and sword for all to see. In perfect English he would shout at us, telling us what great things were being done by his race, how the English had been disgraced and that the Nipponese were now our masters.

CHAPTER

|✳|✳| 9 |✳|✳|

LIVING WITH THE NUNS

IN 1942–3 when we must have been living in this group of houses for almost a year, we were on the move once again. As we were on the outskirts of the town, it must have been difficult for the Japs to keep us under surveillance, so this time we were moved to a house called Silver Oaks which in the pre-war days had been a boarding house kept by a Miss Harding. It was set up on a hill cut into terraces with wide paths divided by handsome brick steps. A crescent-shaped drive connected the two gates which opened on to the main road and in this crescent was a large covered well. Now we really were squashed, all fifteen of us, ten nuns, two servants and the three of us children. The Japs must have been living there before us, because they left us amply supplied with air-raid shelters dug into the terraces. It was possible to stand up in them and, had we known what was to come, we could have made them tolerably comfortable, in spite of the seeping mud walls.

Once again we had a very large compound full of orange and lime trees which in the early morning would be strung with cobwebs stretching from one tree to the next, giving the impression of a whole compound glistening with precious jewels. The spiders spinning these webs were evil-looking and not at all enticing. A huge jacaranda tree grew quite close to the house on one side, and just outside the gate on the upper level grew tamarind trees and groves of bamboo. Behind the house the ground sloped down gently, while on the remaining side was dense jungle.

The largest room, which was on the second storey, was given over to the chapel and all the nuns save three slept in rooms on the same floor. On the ground floor slept Teresina, Aridiem Mary, Sister Antonietta, and the three of us in one room – a terrible squash. Sister Esterina (chronically ill and requiring constant nursing by Sister Antonietta) occupied the adjoining room. Sister Marie-Louise, who was in charge of Teresina and Aridiem Mary, the kitchen, and Bobby and Fido the dogs, slept in one of the back rooms. The kitchen was a large ramshackle lean-to and just a few yards from it were the hen runs and stack of logs for firewood. In the covered porch which was well protected from the weather stood the piano. This porch was regarded as our school room cum dining room cum music room, as well as the visiting room whenever the Japs appeared. From it also we could see all that moved on the road, and thus we had warning of unannounced arrivals. But anyone arriving by the upper gate on the side of the house often took us by surprise.

For the first time since the invasion we were all under the

same roof. Living in such close proximity afforded us a degree of familiarity with the nuns never dreamt of in the pre-war years. The Mother Superior was Mother Irma. Looking wise and kind, she did not have a great deal to do with us in the ordinary course of events, as she did not teach or supervise us. Once in a while, though, we felt she was observing each of us in turn as though summing up our strengths and weaknesses. Whoever was the object of her scrutiny would be aware of her unflinching gaze as we played in the evenings, but she let us get on without interference, even if we quarrelled or became boisterous. Her gaze, however, never made us uncomfortable, only rather thoughtful, holding us back from being too spiteful or nasty to each other. She had much medical knowledge and treated my sores, sometimes a little impatiently, for no sooner did one heal up than another appeared somewhere else, and she nursed Lucy and Mary safely through their frequent bouts of malaria.

Next in command was Sister Erminia, tall, stately and vastly superior in intellect to the rest of the nuns. With her long slightly horsey intelligent face, her mind seemed to be above all the minor irritations that beset us, and our misdemeanours affected her not one bit. She had been an engineer before becoming a nun and she was a wonderful teacher who held our entire attention and was never cross with us. But we loved her most for her story-telling, as her grave unhurried voice held us spellbound. Tales of bravery, and self-sacrifice filled many an evening, one of her favourite authors being C. M. Yonge. Once the story was over a deep, satisfying thoughtfulness would prevail, then digging deep into her pockets and bringing out a pair of scissors, she would cut out paper dolls and animals all joined together. Having no toys whatsoever we treasured these greatly and looked forward to being in her charge, for despite enjoying a generous amount of freedom, we were never left unsupervised for long.

Sister Christine was from Goa, of Anglo-Indian extraction. Also tall and stately she was the darkest-skinned of us all, apart from the Tamil girl, Aridiem Mary. Her consuming passion was for all things English – language, literature, songs, and especially the Royal Family. Her knowledge of the latter was almost intimate, dating from Queen Victoria and her numerous offspring. She knew all their names, as well as those who had married into the family. Resenting the fact that we were lighter skinned than her, especially since we did not seem to appreciate it, she nagged us constantly about going out in the blazing sun without hats or protection of any sort. Assuring us that we would one day be restored to our parents and move about in social circles once more, she felt it her duty to teach us about etiquette, visiting cards, the correct use of knives and forks (for we now ate with our fingers) and how to make polite conversation. How she loved to tell us about her own family, especially about her seven brothers, her voice growing warm and tender when mentioning a favourite one called Charles who was a major in the British army.

She was addicted to Dickens and it was her delight to tell us stories out of *David Copperfield* and *Bleak House*, then make us memorise who were the main characters. Sometimes she would pencil whole paragraphs which she thought beautiful and which we would have to learn by heart and repeat to her. One of them went: 'As I turned the corner I stood spellbound at the beautiful scene. Tucked in the corner of the wood was a cosy-looking red-tiled cottage. No sound came from within, but the smoke spiralling from the chimney bespoke life.' I don't know where this piece came from but it epitomised for me something I was sure must be essentially English, for we sometimes played with jig-saw puzzles depicting such scenes. It saddened her that we had so little appreciation for the things she loved. Sister Christine could sometimes be malicious and hurtful, and she was a dreadful snob, but she instilled in us a great love of both the written and spoken word. Words to her were like precious stones in a treasure chest which she loved to take out and admire, polish and arrange to her entire satisfaction.

Having a very pleasant voice, she sang us songs remembered from the First World War, such as 'Pack up your troubles', 'Tipperary', 'Roses of Picardy', and two little-known ones called 'The Red Cross Nurse' and 'Joan of Arc'. Words such as 'love', 'sweetheart', 'darling', came up fairly frequently in these songs and we were uncomfortable with them sung by a nun. To hide our embarrassment we giggled uncontrollably and, scolding us for being so silly, she would explain to us that the soldier was singing such songs to his mother or sister. It just wasn't done to speak of any other kind of love!

We sensed that she was not generally liked by the other nuns. Because she was so bookish and impractical they took a wicked delight on ironing days as they watched her struggle with her bonnets. As I grew older and came to a better understanding of things, I realised that Sister Christine more than any other nun knew what our European fathers really hoped and expected of us; educated, polished and able to mix in any society. But it was an uphill struggle, as we were not the least bit appreciative of her hard work and gave her no encouragement.

Sister Antonietta was in total charge of us, responsible for our behaviour and well-being and she also gave us music lessons. She loved us fiercely and woe betide anyone who found fault with us or made us unhappy. She was the nearest we had to a mother and we loved her in return, turning to her when we simply had to talk about our anxiety for our parents. Sometimes it did indeed become unbearable, when we wondered if we would ever see them again. Because nobody knew when Lucy and Mary's birthdays were, Sister Antonietta invented special feast days which they celebrated as their birthdays. This gave her an excuse for making a great fuss over them and spoiling them as much as our circumstances permitted. Tiny, pink-faced and doll-like, she did the work of someone twice her size. The nursing demands made on her by the acutely ill Sister Esterina took their toll for she often looked quite washed out. Then we genuinely tried to be as good as possible, polishing the chapel floor until it gleamed the way she liked it, or making a bigger effort to do our piano practice in the way she wanted.

First there were the scales, major and minor, melodic and harmonic, also chromatic and in contrary motion, as well as arpeggios. Then the études, usually by Bach and Scarlatti and Clementi. Only then could we go on to more pleasurable pieces, such as the little Italian shepherd boy tune. Sister Antonietta never seemed to have the time to play for her own pleasure. Instead she would go through all the music books in our possession and play pieces she thought we might like to learn. Lucy always chose the more demanding and fiendishly difficult ones, whereas the sad and wistful ones had a special appeal for me. Mary on the other hand went straight for the jolly, uncomplicated pieces.

With Sister Antonietta we were allowed to talk quite freely and the nun's habit was no impediment if she wanted to give us a hug for good behaviour or to enjoy a good joke. She was responsible for arranging all the music in church and loved

1
My father and mother. The
first photograph of her
shows her in formal
Burmese dress, the second
as I remember her.

2
My father's work as
Assistant Superintendent
took him out into the villages
and into daily contact with
the tribal people who used
also to come down to Kalaw
to barter goods.

3

My mother with jasmine in her hair. She had little idea of how to manage European dress. My sweater must have come from Ireland.

4

I did not enjoy my school uniform, although was happy
when my father made one of his very rare visits.

5

My grandparents' village house was built on stilts like these and I went collecting firewood with my grandfather in a bullock cart like this. Though both pictures were taken recently, very little has changed.

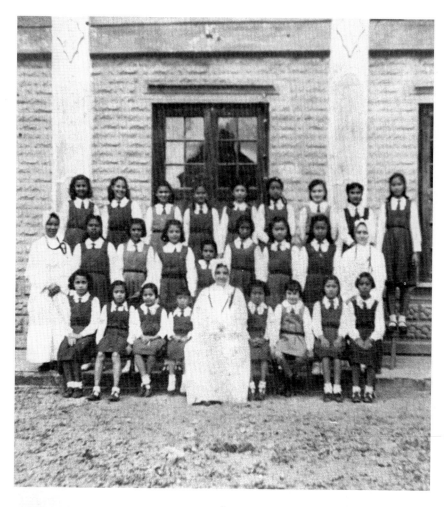

6

St Agnes Convent, rebuilt after the war, with the nuns in their cool-season habit: (*from left to right*) Sister Wilhelmina, Mother Irma, and Sister Antonietta. I am in the top row, second from the left; Lucy Grey is top row centre and Mary Grey centre row, third girl from the left. The smallest girls in the front row were those I had to look after.

7

(*Right*) Andy, the handsome
Dane we were all in love with.
(*Below*) Roy Ogden, who came
to find me at the convent.
(*Below right*) Got up to kill by the
nuns – hardly the right gear for
the high life in Rangoon.

Glengara Park.
Glenageary.
Co Dublin.

April 10th 1943.
Saturday.

My dear Maureen. I hope this letter reaches
you, as we have not heard from you
for over a year, we often get letters
from Daddy, but he has not heard.
If you either and we are very anxious
about you. I got my holiday last
Wednesday, April 7th 1943, I am with Granny &
Valerie my cousin, who is four years old.
This letter I know wont reach you
in time for your birthday, but I hope
you will have had a nice one, you
will have two figures on your age now
instead of one. I am sorry that I cant
send you anything. My birthday is on
this coming Monday I will be twelve (12)
I took some photos of Valerie yesterday
morning. one up in the apple tree, one of her
in her school uniform, and one of her
drawing. Granny is very busy packing
as we are going to live in Glengatown

Valerie is out in the garden now, singing,
she cant really talk properly, like she says
" ME BUY BAR TOC FOR MUMMIE "which really
means' I buy bar of chocolate for Mummum.
I hope you will write to me soon.
Lots of love and kisses
from
OXOXOXOXOX OX Patricia XOXOXOXO

8
The shattering revelation of a
family in Ireland came with
this first letter from my sister.
(*Left*) Pictured with my newly
found sister, at the start of a
new life in Ireland – and out
of uniform at last.

trying out different Masses with difficult part-singing. Her face
would glow with pleasure and she would nod encouragement as
we achieved better and better results. The loving memory of
Sister Antonietta remains one of my childhood's strongest, our
only bulwark against the cruel war which cut across our lives
and deprived us of the love and presence of our families.

Sister Marie-Louise (the same who befriended me in earlier
days) was someone to be reckoned with, as the other nuns
found. Having supreme charge of the kitchen, she allowed no
one in it without good reason, gave working instructions to the
mali, and carried out the bargaining with or without benefit of
interpreters when the village folk came down from the hills
with their produce for barter. For it was now all done by barter,
it being well acknowledged that the Japs printed their own
money, making it worthless. For some time past the nuns had
been kept busy making *eingyis* and *longyis*, using the linen tablecloths left in our safe-keeping by the Kalaw Hotel when the
British were fleeing. These garments were bartered for basic
provisions such as rice and cooking oil. It was to Sister Marie-
Louise that Aridiem Mary would go with tales of any slights,
real or imaginary, and the nun concerned would get a terrible
lashing of Marie-Louise's tongue. With us she was chatty,
understanding and quite unlike some of the other nuns, insisting that we should be allowed to play rather more than pray, and
making snide remarks in the hearing of Mother Superior that
we were being brought up like little nuns rather than normal
children. She was also the only person who, with Aridiem Mary,
could control Bobby, our extremely fierce Irish terrier who
could not abide Japanese soldiers and attacked them savagely
unless restrained.

The youngest sisters were Anita, Annetta and Seraphina (not

the one who had terrorised me in the first standard – she had been sent elsewhere before the Japs arrived). They were probably in their late twenties and early thirties. Sister Anita, slim and graceful, sewed beautifully and took us for needlework. She tried hard to teach us to sew, to turn up a neat hem, or make handkerchieves with drawn-threadwork, and embroider with stem-stitching, leaving mending and darning to the last. But we were hopelessly inept, and unwilling; our efforts were discouraging and turned out grubby and stained, almost reducing her to tears of frustration.

Sister Annetta was a red-faced disapproving nun with a wounding tongue; luckily we had little to do with her, as we did not like her and did not think that she would improve upon longer acquaintance.

Sister Seraphina (the younger) was a lovely, cheerful person. The most remarkable thing about her was her voice which was quite unlike anything I had ever heard. Listening to her singing in church was to bring to mind pictures of pure sparkling waterfalls and birds soaring upwards into the sky. Totally devoid of false modesty or affectation she sang freely, whether in church or, on the rare occasions when, overcome with longing for home or perhaps because of a feast day, the nuns would gather around the piano and sing their hearts out. There was a particular song called 'Juanita' which they sang in Italian, as they did all the other songs, so we never knew what they were singing about. On these occasions I felt very privileged to be allowed to hover at the edge of the circle, and as they sang I wondered what these nuns had left behind in Italy, and whether they ever wished they were back there.

Sister Wilhelmina must surely have been Shan or Chinese or a mixture of both. Young and very attractive, there was something that set her apart from the rest of the nuns which I could not define. Was it a smile of gentle derision which sometimes hovered around her lips as she watched the younger nuns at recreation? Perhaps it was because she had not been fully professed and was still a novice that made her stand out from the others. Sometimes there was such a far-away dreamy look in her shining black eyes that I wanted to ask what she was thinking about. But of course I would never have dared. Like Sister Seraphina's, her voice was also beautiful and the combination of them singing at High Mass (which we still managed to celebrate) was an intoxicating experience.

There remained only two more nuns. Sister Esterina, now chronically ill, was confined to her room next to ours, tenderly nursed by Sister Antonietta. Before her illness she was the most skillful dressmaker I had ever seen. A sweet patient smile hovered around her lips as she fitted us out in Burmese clothes as a present from Mother Superior in the early days of the occupation. It gave her so much pleasure to see that her work had made us so happy. Now, at times when her suffering became unbearable, she would let out a low moan which would make us sit up in our beds. On these occasions Sister Antonietta would drop everything and get into action. Summoning help from Mother Irma she would vanish into the kitchen, soon reappearing with a cloth-covered dish. Aridiem Mary knew what was under the cloth but was only prevailed on to tell us what it was when she had extracted a promise from us that we would help her with the washing up for a whole week so that she could have more time with an admirer. It was a piece of meat, she said, which was laid on Sister Esterina's festering stomach wound so that the cancer would devour it and give the poor nun some relief. When there was a respite from her suffering Father Boldrini would take her the sacrament, but more than once he had been summoned to carry out the last rites of Extreme Unction.

Finally, there was a very old and frail nun, partly senile. It was easy to see that she must have been very pretty when young for she had the bluest eyes we had ever seen, and skin like Dresden china. Always with a smile on her face she was happy just to be able to watch all that happened around her, and often had to be guided to the refectory or chapel or stopped from straying out of the compound.

On feast days and holidays, the nuns could be coaxed into showing us precious photographs of their families. Some of them were so strange to our eyes that we could scarcely refrain from giggling, so different were they from anything we had seen in our villages, the children with unflattering hair cuts and grown-ups with such old-fashioned clothes. It was then also that we learnt some of the nuns' surnames, that Mother Irma's was Corvi, meaning crow, Sister Antonietta's was Cantu, a town in northern Italy, and the most beautiful we thought was Sister Anita's which was Restelli. Sister Christine's was Phillips which was quite familiar to us.

On the whole the nuns coped fairly well with their changed life style, except for one thing – adjusting to life without WCs and making do with the latrine at the bottom of the compound. In their voluminous robes they must have found these somewhat of a trial. At night they made use of chamber pots and with wicked glee we watched them as they disposed of the contents in the morning. The practical ones like Sister Antonietta and Sister Marie-Louise made no bones about it, not the least bit self-conscious. The nuns living on the top floor, however, had to cope with a perilous descent down the long rickety back stairs, holding on to the shaky bannister with one hand, pot in the other, at the same time manoeuvring their petticoats to avoid falling headlong to the bottom. We took great delight watching their expressions, the senior nuns trying to retain some dignity, while the younger tried to cover their embarrassment.

Our move to Silver Oaks had also meant a move for Father Boldrini and his retinue a few hundred yards from us. He was never afraid to speak out against the harsh treatment meted out to prisoners and people the Japs suspected, so they must have found him a thorn in their sides. Twice he was taken away at bayonet-point, but he returned to his house and kept up his work, quite unrepentant. When he sang, intoning the 'Gloria in Excelsis Deo' or the 'Credo in Unum Deum' his voice flowed effortlessly with the golden light and warmth of his native Italy.

Not very far from Father Boldrini lived the Good Shepherd nuns, an Irish community who had also been moved from their own convent. They often told our nuns how lucky they were to have young children like us around. Some of ours agreed wholeheartedly, others managed a polite smile, while one or two looked quite pained. Thursday was set aside as the day on which Father Boldrini said Mass at *their* convent and thus it was that we made the acquaintance of the six Danes.

CHAPTER

|✻|✻| 10 |✻|✻|

TEA PARTIES AND DAILY CHORES

THE DANES LIVED very near the Irish nuns and as we walked to and from Mass on a Thursday we would see six tall European men, wearing shorts, smiling down at us from their compound. Seeing them reminded us of our fathers – jogging our memories in which, with the passing of time, they were becoming shadowy, dim figures, not easily brought into focus. It wasn't long before the Danes struck up conversation with our nuns, and it transpired that one of them, a Mr Andersen (later to be known as Andy), had known Mary and Lucy Grey's father, Wilfred Grey, at Steel Brothers while he and some of the other Danes had been employed by the similar East Asiatic Company. The Danes had been rounded up and interned by the Japanese while trying to escape to India and had a terrible time in Myitkyina before being allowed to settle in Kalaw.

To our amazement and delight we were invited to have tea

with them on a Sunday afternoon – without the nuns! Sister Antonietta set herself the task of making us look as presentable as possible, scrubbing and brushing till it hurt. Obedient children though we were, we nevertheless protested strongly when she wanted to tie ribbons in our hair, as in those photographs of Italian children we had so recently seen and giggled at. Our dresses were plain, shapeless and almost shabby, but clean. We had long outgrown our shoes and the clogs with which they had been replaced would no longer hold the broad leather strap fixed to them by an assortment of nails. Walking barefoot in the cold mornings was painful as the skin on our heels cracked and never seemed to heal up, but there was no alternative. Sister Antonietta had to be satisfied with her work on us and after a lecture from Sister Christine on etiquette and suggestions for conversation topics, we left with Sister Antonietta, full of excitement and anticipation.

We were completely awe-struck when the six Danes came to greet us at their gate, especially when we realised that Sister Antonietta was waving us good-bye. For the first time we were completely without nuns and we looked at each other wondering what to say and do, Sister Christine's very recent instruction quite evaporating. Our hosts could see we were overcome with shyness and more comfortable sticking together, so they showed us around their beautiful garden which seemed to be the work of Mr Olsen. Then Mr Ibsen and Mr Andersen showed us the hen houses which took us by surprise. For we had never seen such beautifully crafted and immaculately clean runs, where both chicks and ducks were penned. Everything was meticulously tidy and the hens had special nesting boxes, not like ours at Silver Oaks, where we had to search for hours to try and find where the wretched creatures had laid their eggs.

Someone suggested a game of Pass the Ring and I Spy. Still a little shy, we settled into deck chairs and waited for the game to start. It was my misfortune to land on a chair which had a slight rent in the canvas, but I was far too afraid to admit the fact in case it was reported to the nuns. So I perched very cautiously and it was with great relief when I moved one seat to the left in the course of the game, and the suspect deck chair was next occupied by one of the men. But not for long, as he was taken completely by surprise, his bottom hitting the ground, while his legs shot up in the air. There was uproarious laughter at the ridiculous spectacle, the ice was broken and we started to enjoy the afternoon.

It was now time for tea which was set out on a long table covered with a snowy white cloth in another part of the garden. Our jaws dropped in amazement. For the table was laden with food the likes of which we had not seen for a very long time – cakes and buns, tiny sandwiches and biscuits which all looked so tempting that it was an effort not to reach out and grab something. But of course we remembered our manners and sat down as demurely as we could. Only then did we see that we each had a boiled egg in an egg cup and the Danes were waiting for us to start. How were we to eat our eggs? Hadn't Sister Christine told us that there was a right way and a wrong way to eat a boiled egg? And we had not been paying attention, so now we didn't know. What a golden opportunity we were missing to put into practice one of her lessons on how to conduct ourselves in company! The Danes asked us kindly whether we didn't like eggs and we replied that we did, although we had not had them for ages and had forgotten what they tasted like. They looked encouragingly at us, we looked hopelessly at each other for inspiration, terrified that when Sister Christine asked us what we had for tea, as she most certainly would, she interrogated us on how we had eaten our eggs. Not knowing what to do, we left the eggs untouched and the Danes were mystified!

Luckily the Danes seemed to enjoy our company, for we were asked to tea many times (without eggs!) and looked forward greatly to our visits. How we fought among ourselves to try and sit next to Mr Andersen, the handsomest of the lot, with his piercing blue eyes and golden hair. But we liked Mr Castonier, the Danish Consul as well, although Mr Castonier's enormous height intimidated us a little, as it did the Japanese, which was why he had been singled out for preferential treatment and had suffered brutal beatings and humiliation at their hands before being allowed to come and settle in Kalaw. Looking back to those happy afternoons now I find it very touching that those great big and important men could be so wonderfully kind to three insignificant little girls and devote so much time to their happiness. For there was gentle rivalry amongst them as they took it in turn to prepare all the good things we had to eat, asking us, in fun, whose tea we liked the best.

We used to wonder how they were able to obtain such marvellous goodies, for we never saw anything like that with the nuns at Silver Oaks. We came to the conclusion that the Danes were just that much cleverer than poor Sister Marie-Louise. What we did not know then was that the Danes had a great deal of money at their disposal, all the East Asiatic Company's money in fact, which had been hidden in a deep hole dug where the chickens were kept. No wonder it all looked so clean and tidy! As well as that, they had loyal servants who had means at their disposal.

By 1944 we were beginning to think that the war would go on forever. I was now eleven years old, and Lucy, Mary and I had been making the best of each other's company for three years. No two sisters could have been more unalike. Lucy, pale-skinned and round-faced, had an enormous amount of hair which was black and frizzy, and could almost have passed for Chinese in those days. As well as being good at maths she was also an expert at playing Bach and how I envied her expertise and her strong left hand on the piano. Even at theory she had no difficulty. Mary was very pretty, with brown hair and eyes and a rosy complexion, very European-looking. She was very much under Lucy's thumb, but she and I nevertheless got on very well together, when Lucy allowed it. Mary was a great favourite with the nuns because of her looks, but she could be good fun and ready for any escapade.

On one occasion I spotted a great bulbous thing hanging from the eaves on one side of the house. Not knowing what it was, Mary and I decided to investigate and went in search of long bamboos with which to dislodge the curious object. A bit of prodding brought the thing down – as well as hundreds of extremely irate hornets! Mercilessly seeking vengeance, they covered us both, embedding their stings into our faces, necks, arms and legs. Our terrified screams brought Lucy and Fido the dog to the scene, and they in turn drew the same horrific but undeserved retribution on themselves. Through our almost sealed eyes we caught a glimpse of poor Fido on whom the hornets stuck like brooches and his yelping was piteous to hear. When the nuns found us we were in a desperate state, unable to see, in agonising pain, faces red and swelling alarmingly. That we got through the next week was due entirely to their skillful nursing, for we were often delirious and unconscious for a lot of the time. When finally we recovered it was to a severe scold-ing (deservedly in the case of Mary and me) from all the nuns, including Sister Antonietta, usually so sympathetic, who made us promise always to leave things alone, a promise readily undertaken!

Fiercely competitive at the piano, we regarded the pieces we played as uniquely our own and woe betide anyone caught playing someone else's. One such piece was a lovely Italian air with a little shepherd boy on the cover playing the flute while sheep grazed peacefully. Whenever Lucy was out of the room and out of earshot Mary and I would rush to the piano and try to memorise as much of it as possible. But our renderings never sounded quite the same as Lucy's, for she played faultlessly and easily. We still played a lot of trios and duets, Lucy usually playing the treble, Mary in the middle and me playing the bass parts. By now the nuns who had been raiding the trunks left by the Kalaw Hotel had come across lots of sheet music, mostly love songs and popular music, giving us an insight into what the wicked outside world enjoyed.

Because Mary and I were much more European-looking than Burmese the nuns sometimes feared for our safety. It was on this account that whenever a Japanese appeared in our midst Mary and I were hidden away and Lucy would be paraded as a token pupil. Only if the visitor was deemed safe were Mary and I brought out of hiding to be presented as part of the community also. Our piano-playing proved to be very useful as a diversionary tactic on these occasions. For, as times worsened, the Japanese would often send soldiers in search of whatever could be had to take away by force, such as chickens and ducks. Hastily, we would be summoned, cleaned up and plonked on the piano stools in the front room with the Japanese soldier, while the nuns chased the chickens and ducks into the jungle.

One day we were in for a surprise. A soldier came and was

seated as usual and after a certain amount of quarrelling about what to play we settled down to perform our set pieces. Curious to see what effect our playing was having on him, I turned around to have a peep. I was flabbergasted. There he sat, a rough-looking chap, tears flowing silently down his face, while he gazed at a snapshot cradled in his yellow palms.

Nudging Mary with my elbow I hissed, 'Tell Lucy he's crying!'

To which she hissed back, 'Don't be stupid.' Nevertheless she also turned round to see for herself.

'What shall we do? Shall we stop?' asked Mary.

'No,' said Lucy, 'keep going.'

But it was difficult to do so and our playing soon trickled to a stop. The soldier beckoned to us and we stood cautiously on either side of his chair. Pointing a stubby finger at the photograph, he showed us a formal picture of a Japanese woman and two children, a boy and girl standing stiffly beside her – his family? Without saying a word, he returned the photograph to his breast pocket and, patting each of us on the head, left quietly.

The unusual thing about this soldier, apart from the tears, was he did not smell quite the same as most of the other soldiers when they stood near us. It was this lack of a smell that made us unafraid of him, for sometimes the Japs smelt threatening and harmful – a very difficult sensation to define.

No sooner had he left than in bustled Sister Marie-Louise with two of the scrawniest chickens she could find, one under each arm. Her face was an absolute picture when she saw the departing Japanese soldier and heard what we had to tell her. Shaking her head in disbelief, she went out to release the chickens. This was a side of the Japanese I had not seen before and it made me wonder whether they were not so different from other people after all.

In the evenings they would sing as they marched in long columns past our house and we would watch them while their voices rang out, repeating each line twice. They had quite a repertoire, the tunes were easy and, despite their guttural voices, very catchy. What were they singing about, I wondered, finding it easy to put myself in their place, so far away from home and family. Perhaps even they could be homesick I thought, feeling a tiny bit sorry for them. The nuns, however, thought the songs sounded too warlike for anything of the sort but, the tunes being so catchy, we sang them when the nuns were not around. About two years ago at a dinner party I recounted this memory to a couple of Japanese guests, father and teenage son, humming part of one of the marching songs. To them it was instantly recognisable and with a smile they told me that it was a well-known nursery rhyme! Of course, we didn't know what words the soldiers sang to the tune.

One day the Japs decided that we would have to work for them. Oranges grew plentifully in Kalaw, there were large groves of them. Huge baskets were brought to us daily and it was our job to peel and cut them up, to be collected in the evening. A long row of tables was set up in the front of the house under the jacaranda tree, and we were set to work with the nuns, but in the process we three greedy children consumed so many oranges that we were miserably sick during the night. After two weeks or so the Japs decided to end our employment. We never discovered what they did with the cut fruit.

We were now feeling the effects of the war more severely. Despite the nuns' industry and economy we were beginning to run out of clothes, and our store of food was being depleted.

Money was non-existent and worthless anyway. Our sole source of food consisted of trade with the hill people who travelled great distances up and down steep mountains to sell their produce in Kalaw open-air market. They would pour in like beasts of burden, their backs bent under the enormous baskets of fruit, tobacco, eggs, chickens, ducks, rice and vegetables. These baskets, sometimes with a smaller one on top, were suspended from a strap across their brows. Alongside the sturdy woman (for they were almost always women who carried these loads) paced little daughters bearing their smaller siblings on their backs. It was usually the woman who conducted most of the business in the market place, the men spending their time sitting about smoking and gambling.

These picturesque hill people would turn up without warning at any time of the day. One of us would tell Sister Marie-Louise of their arrival and, with Aridiem Mary or Teresina in support, the goods would be inspected before the serious business of bartering commenced. Sitting on their hunkers they kept up a perpetual chatter in sing-song nasal voices, chewing betel nut all the while and spitting out the disgusting red residue from time to time. It didn't matter that Sister Marie-Louise could not speak their language, for they spoke a mixture of several dialects and could not be understood even by Aridiem Mary or Teresina, herself a Karen. But it was amazing how well we all got on just by sign language and facial expressions.

The Padaung women were the most distinctive of all with their elongated necks, considered a mark of great beauty. These were supported by numerous silver collars which a girl started to wear as soon as feasible with more being added as she grew. Similar rings would decorate her calves and ankles and, as if this weight were insufficient, three or four silver bangles would be clasped around each wrist, heavy earrings spiked through her ears and silver pins adorn her black hair. As well as Padaungs there were Palaungs, Kachins, Karens and Taung-thus, but it was not always easy to distinguish one tribe from another. Some had coils of thin bamboo cane around their waists, others had silver coils around their legs below the knees, while some simply wore puttees. Often the lobes of their ears would be distended by the enormous silver pendants which hung from them. They wore a variety of headgear which, although simple, always added to their graceful bearing.

It was easy to tell at what point the bartering was becoming difficult for Sister Marie-Louise, for it was then that she would order Aridiem Mary or Teresina to fetch the clothes, beautifully made by the nuns out of the hotel linen, so carefully unpicked by us in order to save the thread which was needed for resewing. Only Aridiem Mary and Teresina would be allowed to handle the *eingyis* and *longyis* which the hill people would buy, not for themselves, for they wore different clothes, but for bartering with the Burmese. If they thought Sister Marie-Louise was striking a hard bargain the hill people would pack up and go, but not too far away. We would see them lingering at the gate, hoping to be called back. They seldom were, but if so, they would come back to renegotiate calmly enough at first, then the nods and head-shakes accompanied by emphatic raising and lowering of the arm would get more urgent until final agreement could be reached without loss of face on either side. Satisfied with the day's proceedings, which brought us much needed kerosene oil as well as food, they would depart, to appear again within the next few weeks. These people often came with rumours of how things stood with the Japanese but the nuns realised that it would be unwise to rely too much on the news they imparted, and were careful not to react at all in their presence, for we never knew whether we were being reported.

In the trunks containing the damask napkins there were also some beautiful dresses which the nuns cut up for us, but the resulting effect was rather comical worn without shoes, and totally unsuitable for chasing chickens in the jungle or carrying water. For by now we had to work harder than ever. Our well had dried up, so water had to be fetched from a neighbour's some distance away. This was the most arduous task of all for Mary, Lucy and me. We had to lift up two tall full-sized kerosene oil cans filled to the brim (at the start of the trip, anyway), spilling a lot on the way and blaming each other for so doing. Every day all the receptacles in the kitchen and bathrooms had to be filled and it took several trips, quite exhausting us for anything else. In former times the *mali* would have dealt much more efficiently with this chore, but he had been dismissed for stealing spare mattresses and mosquito nets. Also firewood had to be gathered, the house kept clean, and the straying chickens kept in control. No wonder lessons were dispensed with.

It was about this time that I was plagued with bad dreams, dreams in which both my parents died. The nightmares about my mother always involved the evil *nats* she had warned me about who lived in banyan trees, while the dreams of my father strangely seemed to take place in a hospital in Calcutta. Perhaps we had been studying India in geography. I had no idea where my father was and as far as I knew he was still somewhere in Northern Burma. But the dream was very vivid; he was in a hospital bed lying under a white sheet, looking very pale, and there was a nurse putting a finger to her lips, cautioning me to be quiet. Trying to comfort me, Sister Antonietta would say that dreaming of death meant one would live for a long time, but I could not shake off the heavy load which seemed to settle on my shoulders.

Little by little we noticed an influx of Japanese women into the neighbourhood. Their faces chalk white and moonlike, they were very fat with robust legs, unsmiling expressions, and always dressed in white. We wondered what they were here for and the nuns told us they were nurses who had come to look after the soldiers. Not quite believing them, we asked Aridiem Mary who just gave us a broad wink, but the same question to Teresina resulted in a painful clout on our heads for 'asking questions about which we had no business'!

CHAPTER

|✳|✳| 11 |✳|✳|

NUNS AND GUNS

Up to now in early 1945 we more or less had freedom of movement, so long as we kept away from restricted places. We had become accustomed to the sudden arrival of soldiers in our midst which we construed to be their way of keeping up appearances. But one day we were rounded up by several of them and given orders by a Japanese officer that from now on we would no longer have the freedom to go in and out of our compound. This was because Italy had surrendered to the Allies, therefore we would now be regarded as enemies and were to consider ourselves interned. Our situation had changed quite suddenly. Anxious looks were exchanged for we *had* to go out of our compound to fetch water. Surprisingly, we were still allowed to do this, but we knew we were being closely watched and that we would have to be careful.

We did not need any telling that a change was taking place in the war. At night the sky in the distance was lit up and flares brightened the darkness. Searchlights made such a beautiful sight and we clapped our hands in delight, not realising that they meant destruction and death. For the nuns reckoned that the town of Heho, twenty-two miles distant with its airstrip, was being bombed as the planes droned in night after night. But we were completely unaware of the load of destruction they were carrying. Soon we were seeing aircraft flying over us in the daytime, not Japanese because they did not have the red sun emblem painted on the underside of the wings. Quite unafraid, we would run out and count them as they swooped low overhead. We were very excited and wondered what it all meant; only the nuns were cautious, discouraging us from going out into the open when these planes flew over.

Their caution was not without foundation. Without any warning we received our first bombing, and it was terrifying. The blast took us completely by surprise and in a panic we rushed to the centre of the house. Huddling together we screamed, prayed and cried hysterically. Someone tried to count heads to see if anyone was missing. The planes bombed and retreated, then made fresh attacks. All around us furniture crashed and clocks struck crazily. The planes flew so low that we were sure they would rip off the roof. All of a sudden there was silence, a great waiting and eerie silence which we could not trust entirely. In those days there were no screaming ambulances to signal the bombing was over and the task of removing the dead and wounded could begin. It seemed an eternity before Mother Irma at last said that she was going to venture out. She was soon back and we were allowed to leave the room. Outside it was strangely quiet with smoke rising from several places. In the direction of the convent, now occupied by the

Japanese, dense smoke billowed in a black cloud – it looked as though the building had received a direct hit.

The senior nuns made an appraisal of our situation. Standing on the edge of the circle we could hear some of them reckoning that we were now going to be bombed just as Heho had been. The air-raid shelters built into the terracing by the Japanese for their own use would now come in handy for us. Mother Superior and Sister Erminia went down to inspect them. The three of us looked at each other, all thinking exactly the same thing. Like the fruit trees in the garden, the entrances to the shelters were festooned with spiders' webs. The spiders were as big as our hands, brightly coloured, poisonous and frightening, so we had steered clear of the trenches in our games. They also smelt foul and dank, as water seeped from all surfaces, collecting in little puddles on the mud floors. But, as we guessed, we were given the task of getting them ready for occupation, which we did by scraping the ceilings and walls to get rid of debris and sluicing the floor of stagnant water. It was a disagreeable job as we slithered about on the slimy clay in our bare feet. As soon as it was dry, we laid down bamboo matting and brought in two or three stools for the older nuns. While the three of us could stand upright in the trenches, very few of the nuns could because most of them were taller than the Japanese.

The preparation was done none too soon for from that day on we were bombed every day for three months, sometimes two or three times a day. It was pitch black in the trenches because although the entrances, which were about eighteen inches wide and cut at regular intervals, provided a certain amount of light, it was safer to stand well away from them in case shell splinters got in.

As soon as we heard the droning of the planes in the distance we would rush to our shelter, and one nun always made herself responsible for seeing we were all there, except of course Sister Esterina who was confined to bed. Prayers would start immediately, usually the Litany or the Rosary, the voices rising in urgency the nearer the bombs seemed to drop. If Sister Antonietta were present she would envelop the three of us like a guardian angel, keeping our heads covered. As we got used to the raids only the loudest ear-splitting blasts frightened us but the younger nuns were terrified and made a lot of noise about it. Nobody was allowed out until Mother Superior or Sister Erminia gave the signal that it was safe to venture forth. Then we children would rush out to pick up splinters from the shell cases and, competitive as ever, argue about who had found the biggest or the most interesting shape.

The only communication we had with the world outside the compound was with Father Boldrini who challenged both the bombs and the Japanese by coming to say Mass at our place every morning. For a time even the hill people stopped coming to barter with us, and as for having tea with the Danes, that had been stopped for some time. Living in the trenches, however, became routine and we got on with it as best we could.

Though the nuns had raided the chests and trunks entrusted to us for our own survival, they still had a sense of responsibility for the hotel silver and other people's valuables. To leave them in the house by day was considered too risky, for fear of a direct hit. To carry them out of the house in the daytime and bury them in the jungle or camouflage them in the compound seemed to be the only solution. But dacoits were another problem and there were plenty of them about, war or no war, so at the close of each day these chests and boxes had to be dug out and carried back in to the comparative safety of the house.

It fell to us children to perform these tasks. There seemed to be no easy way out. Many a time we tried to carry them as short a distance as possible from the house, only to be told to move them a bit further away for safety sake. How we hated the Kalaw Hotel and all the people who had left their stuff with the nuns. We tried once or twice to 'forget' them in the evening, hoping the dacoits would find the loot, but someone always remembered to do a check. We were frequently reduced to tears of fatigue and vexation and the relentless toil left us with raw, red hands, grazed shins, stubbed toes and downcast spirits.

The bombing was so terrifying that it reduced the four youngest nuns to nervous wrecks and they pleaded with their Superior to be allowed to go deep into the jungle until either the bombing or the war ended. It was no use Reverend Mother pointing out to them that they probably faced greater danger from dacoits, wild animals and malaria in the jungle than from the bombs. Rumours that the Japanese were now retreating added to the hazards of the jungle and must have made Reverend Mother doubly apprehensive, but in the end she capitulated and, against her better judgement, allowed them on their way.

Long after the war was over our Danish friend Mr Andersen told me that the RAF had dropped over four thousand incendiary bombs on Kalaw, one of which landed only two hundred yards from the Danes' house. The situation was indeed becoming extremely dangerous, especially for aliens; at one point it was the Japanese plan to take the Danes out of the town and shoot them, as they were regarded as arrogant, pro-British and spies.

In the meantime we ourselves were receiving news about the Allies' progress from the hill people when they ventured back to barter with us again. At times the news was so exciting it was difficult to contain oneself. When we heard that the British and Americans were only four days away we would be filled with great relief and happiness, but then in two days' time would come the news that they had been pushed back ten days, throwing us into a deep and anxious gloom. But Allied planes were already dropping leaflets announcing their imminent arrival. We could only pick these up at night, as it would have been dangerous to be seen reading them by the Japs. Word had somehow got to the nuns that the Japs were becoming suspicious of us as no bombs had been dropped as near to our house as to some of the other houses. Perhaps we had been signalling to the Allies by hanging washing on the line? So that had to be stopped.

About a week after the young nuns had left to escape the bombing we were surprised to hear a commotion in the front room. They had returned, and what a pathetic sight they presented. Bruised, battered and bleeding, their clothes torn, their bonnets missing, they had escaped after capture by the Japs. Shaken by sobs and frequently breaking down completely, they told of the terrible things that had been done to them. But when their voices descended to a virtual whisper, it was noticed that we children were still present and at this point we were shooed out of the room by Mother Superior. For days after that all the nuns looked very solemn and the young ones took a long time to recover from their ordeal. The situation was now very grave. Added to the daily bombing raids, there was the unmistakable boom of cannon, sporadic at first, but becoming more regular as the days went by. First there was the thud, followed by the piercing arcing whistle overhead, then the resounding thud as the shell landed on its target.

It was only on meeting Mr Andersen again all those years

later that I found out how close we had been to extinction. For putting his arm around me he said, 'You know, Maureen, you and I have been living on borrowed time.' I thought this was said in a general way at first, but he explained how he had learnt after the liberation that the British pilots, flying their planes low over our compound, reported to the ground troops that they had 'seen some nuns'. At first this was misheard as 'seen some guns' and the cannons were trained on us. At the last minute a final check was made and, fortunately for us, 'nuns' rather than 'guns' won the day.

There were other unmistakable signs that things were getting serious. Day and night we were exhorted by the nuns to be good to each other, to forgive and obtain forgiveness for misdeeds. We were always in the habit of rising in the mornings with a prayer on our lips, sleepily muttered, and night prayers rushed through, but now Sister Antonietta would urge us to put some fervour into our night prayers especially, not knowing whether we would survive a night raid. The prayer she especially favoured went:

'Into Thy Hands O Lord, I commend my spirit.
O Lord Jesus receive my soul.
Jesus, Mary and Joseph, I give you my heart and soul.
Jesus, Mary and Joseph, may I bring forth my soul in
  peace, Amen.'

Uncertain what the future held, Mother Superior decided that I should become a Catholic. As I had virtually been brought up as one ever since the beginning of the occupation, it was considered that there was no need for special instruction. Sister Antonietta, beaming delight, said I could choose all the hymns to be sung at my Baptism and First Communion and I chose 'Panis Angelicus' and Gounod's 'Ave Maria'. And so on the morning of Corpus Christi before Mass, with Joseph's daughter Josephine acting as godmother, Father Boldrini received me into the Catholic Church and I made my First Communion during Mass. I was eleven years old, my faith strong in those days, and no inducements were needed. 'Panis Angelicus' sung by Sister Seraphina was ravishing and I wished with all my heart that the singing would go on for ever. All day I felt I was walking in saintliness, probably with an idiotic smile on my face which I hoped would pass for an outward sign of the inward grace which the nuns assured me was now possessing my soul. In my white dress and veil I was excused all chores.

It was a relief to get back to normal the next day and shed my angelic look which hadn't fooled Mary and Lucy for a moment. They were just glad I could do my share of the work again! Nevertheless I now felt less isolated, no longer being left behind while they went up to receive the sacrament.

I remember once being so tired of being left out on my own when Mary and Lucy went to confession, that I decided to make confession myself. But once in the darkness of the confessional I burst into tears because I did not know what I was supposed to do next. Then I poured out my woes about how horrid Lucy was making me do her homework, and how Mary had made a mess which I had had to clean up. All Father Boldrini said was that we should all three come round and see him afterwards and he'd see if he had any sweets for us.

In later life friends and relations tried to make me see that at eleven I had been too young to know what I was doing, and that the nuns had no right to exert such influence over me, but becoming a Catholic was a step I have never regretted taking.

It was now about April or May, 1945. Fewer and fewer of the Japanese soldiers were seen and they had stopped marching past our gate. I missed their singing. There was a strangeness in the air, a sense of unreality and excitement, tinged with an ever-present anxiety. On Easter Sunday Sister Marie-Louise, who refused to be deterred by the bombing, provided us with a festival lunch of chicken, a rare treat in those days. I can still picture the huge *chatties* containing the food being carried down and deposited under the shade of a tree. Dashing out of our trenches we did as much justice to Sister Marie-Louise's cooking as if we were eating in the most peaceful surroundings.

We were surprised at the appearance of a new type of Japanese soldier who sometimes ventured into our compound when it was dark. For the most part on crutches and maimed, some with bandages on their heads or arms in slings, they would beg for water or rice, extending a metal container and slinking off into the darkness afterwards. They were no longer a cause for alarm, we pitied them and the nuns gave them what they could spare. Somehow they gave us to understand that all the hospitals had been closed, leaving the wounded and ill soldiers to fend for themselves as best they could.

One day, looking out from the top verandah, we saw a huddled shape just beyond the compound jumping convulsively and collapsing again. Forgetting our orders not to go out of our grounds, we rushed to the huddle to find it was a dying vulture. We were very excited and picked it up by its wings which were enormously heavy with a span of about six feet. It took all our strength to carry it but we struggled along. All of a sudden its ugly head reared up and with its cruel beak it made a last desperate stab to left and right. We dropped it in fright, picking it up again very gingerly and only when it really seemed to have given up the fight, before lugging it back to the house. What we intended to do with it was not at all clear, but we had some idea that it would make an appetising addition to our boring meals. For some time we had been in the habit of catching sparrows in a long, low, narrow cage, becoming quite adept not only at capturing them, but also at wringing their necks. After plucking they would be skewered and roasted, making a welcome addition to our diet, and we had some idea that the vulture would serve the same purpose. The nuns did not consider the vulture quite such a delicacy however. We were given a sound scolding for being so stupid, and told to kill it and then bury it as far away from the house as possible, and deep enough to prevent it being dug up by pariah dogs. We had to get Aridiem Mary's help with the killing, as we had not the stomach for it. But she was not so squeamish and hacked off its head with a sharp *dah*. In the past she had often got us to help kill chickens, a most unpleasant task, for we had to pin down the poor fowl while Aridiem Mary sawed away at its neck until it was severed. So we felt very dejected at the harsh reception of our good intentions over the vulture. As for pariah dogs, there were not many of these about now. For the past few weeks, as food was running out, they had been caught and slaughtered by the Japanese for their own consumption.

We were made exceedingly bold by our uninterrupted vulture-capturing excursion outside the compound and now ventured further afield. It was easy to escape the attention of the nuns who spent more and more time in the chapel praying. It was exciting but also frightening entering houses formerly occupied by the Japanese, now completely abandoned. In one such house I was overtaken by a powerful sense of having been there before and stopped in my tracks, wondering why it should be so. And then the realisation came to me. I was surprised that I was capable of remembering so much. The house had belonged to the Ogdens in former days and there rose such a vivid picture in my mind's eye of a beautiful lady to whose skirt I clung when I was small, as she walked about the house and garden. I recalled the exact sensations I felt those years ago, when the convent was new and frightening and life was conducted in a foreign language and I thought I might never see my mother or father again. I told Lucy and Mary about this but they were not the slightest bit impressed for they had discovered bags and bags of hard dried beans. Surely the nuns would be glad if we brought back a load of them? We filled our skirts with as much as we could carry, hoping we would not be scolded for stealing, for that was surely what we were doing.

The nuns were certainly pleased and sent us back for more. But the skins were very tough, so they soaked them for a day or two, and then we were shown how to peel them before they could be cooked. Once again we had landed a really disagreeable task. For the smell was intolerable and the taste worse! We had been living on diet of rice, which was fine, and pumpkins which we detested but this new addition of beans was a disaster as far as we were concerned.

Sister Marie-Louise announced one morning that we three children looked peaky, but that she knew of a remedy. There was a white flower growing wild which, boiled and strained and taken twice a day, would soon put the colour back into our cheeks. So out we were sent to fill our skirts with these flowers and bring them back to Sister Marie-Louise. Eagerly we gathered around her for the first spoonful of this wonderful potion, but the taste was vile. She made us persevere, but instead of thriving we became quite ill and so, much to our relief, this dosing was stopped.

While the three of us had been occupied in raiding the empty houses, Aridiem Mary had not been idle. On the pretext of taking Bobby the dog for walks, she stumbled on the most amazing piece of news, and promised to let us into her secret if we helped her in the kitchen. First she took Lucy, being the eldest, with her on her walk. Lucy came back hardly believing what she had seen. For they had witnessed a mass burial of Japanese soldiers, and both of them swore that not all the soldiers had been quite dead, for they had seen some of the bodies twitch. Mary was next to be taken and confirmed their stories. By now the excitement was too much to be contained and the nuns became suspicious. Realising with alarm that Aridiem Mary had made a potentially dangerous discovery, they put a stop to these walks, thus preventing me having my turn as a gruesome spectator.

Now the air-raids were diminishing everyone was anxious to see what had happened to the convent. Deciding that it was safe to do so, two nuns set out one day to find out, taking Lucy with them and their food in a tiffin-carrier. They were away for the whole day and returned very much shaken by what they had seen. On the way there were dead bodies lying unburied, and when they got to the convent they found that it had been very badly bombed, two whole buildings almost totally destroyed. What was especially disturbing was that the playground had also been used for another mass burial. Some of the nuns pleaded for a return to the convent, despite its condition, but luckily common sense prevailed. Mother Superior had concluded that, although the Japanese were supposed to be retreating, there could still be pockets of resistance hiding in the convent and its grounds. The church was only slightly damaged, and because it had seemed fairly intact they did not enter it for that reason.

The nuns were even more cautious now, fearing retaliation by retreating Japanese. Wounded or deserting soldiers still appeared from time to time begging food and water, a pathetic sight. Eventually they stopped coming altogether and an uneasy calm settled over the place.

CHAPTER

|✳|✳| 12 |✳|✳|

LIBERATION AND FAREWELL

WE HAD BEEN TOLD repeatedly just what to do if any strange people were seen around the compound, and that was to run up to the top floor and lock ourselves out on the verandah next to the chapel, keep our heads down and wait to be called down again. It was 8 June at about noon. Noticing some movement at the foot of the hill, we stood rooted to the spot, completely forgetting our instructions. For we saw crawling up the hill on their stomachs, rifles trained in our direction, men not with yellow faces, but bright brick-red ones. Certain that they were British, we threw caution to the winds and beckoned the soldiers on, unable to stop jumping up and down with excitement. We shouted to the nuns that the British had arrived and begged to be allowed to stay downstairs, but they bundled us upstairs where we were still able to peer down at the advancing soldiers through the verandah rails. The soldiers were as cautious as the nuns, edging their way up the hill until they were quite sure that this was friendly territory, and they could enter the house. Now we scrambled downstairs as fast as we could to see the nuns clasping the hands of the soldiers and praising God and all the saints for our deliverance.

The British soldiers asked how long it was since we had seen any Japanese, and producing a map, pored over it with the nuns who were only too happy to point out the focal points. How we stared at them, noting the differences in uniform and colouring, and their strange English voices, so long unheard. Now for the first time and to our complete surprise and delight we heard that the war in Europe was over. But they could not linger, for the nuns had told them of Father Boldrini down the road, the six Danes, and the Good Shepherd nuns a few hundred yards away. Promising to return the next day with some supplies, and assuring us that there would be little fear of retaliation, for no Japanese had been seen for a long time, they left. Despite these assurances, however, two of the nuns stayed up all night keeping watch. Unknown to us soldiers had also been positioned at the bottom of the hill to guard us from possible visits by the Japanese bent on retaliation.

It was difficult to sleep that night. We talked and made plans about what we would do when our parents appeared, as surely they would in the next week or so? It was no use the nuns trying to tell us that it would take a long time for things to be sorted out, but they understood our excitement and humoured us.

Very early next morning we were up and looking for the promised return of the British, so afraid that it had all been a lovely dream. True to their word, they did not keep us waiting. Soon there was a long line of trucks on the road, and as we saw one of them turn up to our house, we ran to greet it. The truck stopped outside the kitchen where a beaming Sister Marie-Louise supervised the unloading of sacks of sugar, rice, flour and a drum of cooking oil. Then the soldiers were off again. From now on they called every day, loaded with all kinds of food in tins, packets and sacks, food we hadn't seen for years such as bacon, butter, margarine, bully beef, sausages, even toothpaste and soap, but best of all sweets and chocolates. Overwhelmed with gratitude, the nuns offered to do their laundry and this was willingly accepted by the officers. They were also offered the use of the chapel, the piano and the harmonium. We were thus kept busy emptying tubs of water and spreading clothes out on the grass to dry and, of course, the inevitable irons had to be heated. It was much more fun now though, and there was always the company of the soldiers who were given the freedom of the place to come and go as often as they pleased. We saw a great deal of two soldiers, Geoffrey with his striking blonde hair which he was forever tossing back from his brow, and his friend, John, an honest reliable corporal who just loved to be around the nuns and us, helping with the heavier tasks.

My memory often flies back to those days, especially when I see a group of soldiers, for it was an exciting time. As the nuns came to know the soldiers better, we were allowed to be taken out for rides in their trucks, jeeps and even in their armoured cars. It was exhilarating driving all over the town, the soldiers taking us wherever we wanted to go, for we had not been in a car of any sort for years. Sister Christine kept asking anyone in uniform whether they had come across her brother Charles, never doubting that one day he would turn up.

It wasn't long before the nuns were begging the British to allow them to open a school. A large building which in former days had been a school for Protestant boys called Kingswood (and used by the Japanese as a hospital) was now available and given to the nuns to run. There was hardly need to advertise their intention as people flocked to the gates, begging the nuns to accept their children, boys and girls who had, like us, all missed three years of schooling. Some of the girls looked very grown-up to us three, but the parents assured the nuns that they were all very tall for their age and were in fact only fourteen years old! The nuns turned a blind eye, all were accepted and schooling began in earnest.

At first there seemed to be an invasion of Persians – Shirazees, Rustumgees, Burjorgees – all wealthy traders in pre-war days who valued education greatly, and were now willing to sacrifice everything for the benefit of their children. One who stood out by her voluptuous good looks and figure was a girl called Marie Burjorgee. To our unsophisticated eyes she was everything the nuns disapproved of as a bad influence on us. She wore lipstick whenever soldiers were around, and knew all the latest songs and dance steps. She also possessed a stash of American magazines over which we pored avidly. Marie Burjorgee ridiculed our pathetic stock of songs, laughing in disbelief when she found out that we thought they were being sung to mothers and sisters. She soon put us right on that score! Saying we needed educating, she taught us a great many more songs, such as 'Roll Out the Barrel', 'You Are my Sunshine', 'Oh, Give me Land, Lots of Land', and 'Coming in on a Wing and a Prayer'. We hung on her every word and even did her homework for her, for Marie had no interest whatsoever in school work, shamelessly taking advantage of our admiration and sometimes behaving almost like royalty. We knew she had a boyfriend called Naseem Khan who would ride past the school on his motor cycle every day. Indeed she made us keep a look-out for him, and altogether we thought she was quite the most glamorous thing we had ever seen. What a difference Marie Burjorgee made to our lives, bringing excitement and a wicked sense of fun entirely missing from convent life. We were her willing slaves, vying to do her favours which she accepted as her due.

One very wet evening as we were all having recreation on the broad verandah of the new school an enormously tall officer appeared in our midst. He was dark-skinned and there was no mistaking who he was.

'Do you have a Sister Christine Phillips here?' he asked.

To which we replied, 'Is your name Charles and are you Sister Christine's brother?'

In absolute astonishment he said, 'Yes, I am, but how do you know?'

We ran to get Sister Christine and her face was a picture when we told her that we thought her brother had come. It was a wonderful reunion and we were very moved as we watched them embracing each other time and time again with tears streaming down their faces. Looking back to that wet day I can see them just as they were, a picture standing out so sharply for its pure unadulterated happiness.

Geoffrey and John were still regular callers and we could not help noticing that the latter always asked for Sister Wilhelmina. To our dismay the two soldiers were one day asked not come to the convent any more, for we had grown very fond of them and looked forward to their visits. Then disaster struck. Sister Wilhelmina disappeared and, although we children had not made the connection, it was rumoured by the servants that she had run away with John. It was unbelievable, for John had so often talked about his wife and children, and Sister Wilhelmina was a nun. The days passed in a heavy gloom and we were forbidden to talk about them, for according to the nuns the two runaways had committed mortal sin. Yet we, loving them both, could not help taking their side, hoping that they would be happy and safe.

About a week after their disappearance, when we were all in bed, we children heard the sound of pebbles being thrown against our window and, going down to investigate, the three of us came face to face with the two fugitives. They looked miserable, wet and weary and asked if we could manage to let them stay the night without the knowledge of any of the nuns. Stealthily we carried a mattress and blankets downstairs and made up a bed for them on the tops of four dressing tables pushed together, then kept watch in turn while they slept. At break of day they departed. We wanted so much to help, but were unable to do any more.

Strange how memory works, for I do not remember seeing Sister Wilhelmina again, but a school photograph, given to me by a friend very much later, shows me in the back row and Sister Wilhelmina among the other nuns in the front. I have no recollection of her returning; she must have just slipped back without fuss or excitement.

It had been June 1945 when the British liberated us, soon to be followed by the Australians and the Americans. Life settled down and the nuns were buoyed up by British promises of help with rebuilding the convent. At the more stabilised pace that followed the rapturous excitement of our deliverance from the Japanese our thoughts returned once more to our parents. My mother's face always came readily to my mind, a picture which remains to this day, but my father had become a dim far figure, not easily remembered. His face would rise before me, but it was almost the face of a stranger, a face I used to look forward to seeing, but with the passing of time now only vaguely recognised. No news whatsoever was forthcoming about either of them and we grew dispirited and anxious. We still did not dare ask the nuns why there was no news or whether any enquiries were being made and naturally we began to think there was something wrong. I can well remember the fear, shadowy at first, but taking firmer hold as days and weeks passed without any news of my parents. It held me in an icy grip, try as I might to throw off the almost suffocating premonition I had. Mary, Lucy and I knew each other too well not to realise that we were all very worried, although we did not bring our worry into the open, for not betraying emotion was something you learnt from nuns.

I still suffered from open sores which had to be treated almost daily, much to Mother Superior's annoyance. To my intense surprise at one of these sessions she announced that news of my mother had come to her, that she had been very ill, and I was to pray very hard if I wanted her to get better. I was to ask no questions for the present, but was just to go away, be a good child and pray hard. This astounding news took my breath away. I longed for a bit more by way of explanation but I had to make the best of it as I was abruptly dismissed. I hugged the information to myself until I felt used to it before excitedly telling Lucy and Mary. They still had no news of their father and little brother John, but generously promised that they would pray very hard indeed for my mother's health. When could I expect the next piece of news to arrive, and where was it coming from? We went over every possibility many times but came to no conclusion.

The next time I went for treatment (within the same week), Mother Superior was solemn: 'You're not praying hard enough – your mother's no better.' Then as though driven by exasperation and finding me and my sores too great a burden she lashed out, 'If you want to die, why don't you pray to God to answer your prayers?' Powerless to reply, I fought back my tears as she continued roughly dressing my sores.

Then on a Sunday less than a week after first being informed about my mother, she asked me to stay behind after Mass because a British officer wanted to see me. I was ushered into the schoolroom for his inspection with two other nuns present. I stood there tensely to attention, but he never met my eye nor said a word to me and I was soon dismissed and told to wait outside. My mind was in turmoil. Why wouldn't he look at me? What did he know? What awful thing had happened? When Mother Irma eventually called me in again the news was shattering. My mother was dead – indeed had died about two years ago and that was all the news for the present. My world fell apart. My hopes had been buoyed up just a week ago, only to be dashed to the ground without any explanation. I could not understand why Mother Irma had given me hope, when all the time she must have known that my mother was already dead.

Five days later Mother Irma wanted to see me again as she had more news for me from the same British officer. This time it was to tell me in a plain bald statement that my father also was dead. After he had trekked to India about a year before, he had died, as I had already dreamt, in a hospital in Calcutta. It was incomprehensible. As though falling into a deep abyss I was overwhelmed with a total sense of loss. So much had happened in the space of a week that it was almost as though I was being hurtled into a vast dense blackness which would never lighten.

There seemed to be nothing in front of me except a deep void.

It was difficult to continue as though nothing had happened but it had to be done. Sister Antonietta comforted me as much as she could, and the other children tried to show by their manner that they understood, and were kind. Lucy and Mary grew grave, wondering whether they would get the same bad news and I felt their support. It was unthinkable that I would never again see my lovely mother with her soft ways, fragrant with the smell of jasmine, sometimes so faint it was no more than a quiver in the air. Unbidden, fragments of her bedtime stories sprang up in my mind, for I had always demanded one story after another. I remembered particularly how she would stall, repeating over and over again the words 'Long, long ago' in different cadences while she was making up a story, hoping I would soon be asleep. I would never again hear her pretty laughter nor look on her innocent pleasure as she adorned herself. I grieved too for those happy days in the village with my mother and grandparents and all my little friends.

As for my father, although he had always seemed rather remote, I knew that he had been part of a life which I would not see again. There were so many questions to which I would probably never get any answers, questions such as why mother did not come to take me home for the Christmas holidays when I was eight years old. Why there was total silence from both my parents and why during those holidays before the first Japanese bomb had dropped on Rangoon, I had been fitted out with all those strange clothes. For some reason I connected my mother's non-coming with those warm clothes made by the tailor which felt so unusually heavy and alien.

Any great display of emotion was frowned on, making it difficult enough to get through the day, but the nights were almost unbearable. Only at night-time could I safely give way to unrestrained grief. Sister Antonietta hearing my sobs would steal out of her cubicle to comfort me, taking the blackness out of the night. The other nuns were kind too, showing their sympathy in the ways they knew, such as giving me special holy pictures which they had treasured for years to put in my prayer book. All but Sister Christine who, as we three knew, could be malicious at times, having an ungenerous spirit and a talent for making everyone feel uncomfortable. She reminded me over and over again that I was now living on charity, owed everything to the nuns, and that I was not like the other children. Indeed when the Red Cross came to visit us, delivering basic items of clothing and necessities such as soap, she would not allow Lucy, Mary and me to label them with our names. 'No,' she said with intentional brutality, 'I'm going to place them together and mark them "Orphans"!'

THE READING OF A WILL

THE BRITISH SOLDIERS were making progress rebuilding the convent, parts of which had been so badly bombed that most of the walls had first to be pulled down. Excitedly we watched them at work replacing walls, roofs, doors and windows. Having seen nothing but destruction in the past few months, it was a marvellous change seeing something positive rising out of the rubble. It was good seeing Chinese carpenters being employed once again, while so recently they had been harassed and hunted. The mounds which had marked Japanese graves were removed, the playground was levelled, and Father Boldrini sprinkled holy water over it. Everything was being done to restore the convent to its former state. New pupils who were being turned away as Kingswood could not take any more were promised places as soon as the convent was ready.

When as much of the convent was rebuilt as was immediately

needed to re-open, the move from Silver Oaks was planned. The nuns, eager to show their gratitude to the soldiers, decided that we should give them a Christmas concert. Lessons gave way to preparations for this and an ambitious programme was put together, including a shortened version of *Julius Caesar*. Sister Christine was in her element. For weeks she wrote, plotted, revised the lengthy soliloquies and the crowd scenes, enlisting the help of all the Persian ladies with the costumes. For they had beautiful coloured saris which would look marvellous as togas. Over and over again we repeated the words, some of us barely able to make sense of what we were spouting but, undeterred, we were made to press on. There was also to be a lot of dancing and the programme was to include such dances as the palais glide, the keel row and a square dance to the tune of 'La Paloma'. There was a Burmese song as well, sung by a group of us wearing Burmese clothes but our mouths gaped when we heard the words, for they were those of a love song, and we wondered if the nuns knew what they meant in English.

The great day dawned and the soldiers, with smiles of anticipation, settled down to enjoy themselves, passing expert eyes over the stage which they had constructed. All went reasonably well and the audience clapped encouragingly. I look back to that day with excruciating embarrassment at my rendition of 'Friends, Romans, countrymen', word-perfect but also perfectly wooden. Yet the soldiers sat politely through it all, never giving a sign of boredom or puzzlement. When at last the concert was drawing to a close all the participating children gathered on or near the stage for the last item which was a speech of thanks to the soldiers by children of the upper school. But it never got under way, for as though by an unseen signal the soldiers with one voice broke out into 'White Christmas'. A few of us had heard this song before, yet the heartache and home-sickness in their voices filled all of us with sadness, and you could hear a pin drop, so silent was the hall at the end of it.

As though determined to shake themselves out of their longing, someone burst into 'Roll Out the Barrel', soon taken up by the rest of them and followed with the well-known 'You Are my Sunshine' and other popular songs, finishing off their repertoire with 'For He's a Jolly Good Fellow' – a novel way of addressing a Mother Superior, but not less heartfelt for all that. Everyone was pleased with the evening's entertainment, even Sister Christine who, magnanimous for once, overlooked any errors. Yet I had difficulty keeping back my tears, as I remembered a poor rough Japanese soldier who not so long ago had shown us a photograph of his own wife and two children, and I thought of the heartache he too must have felt.

Before we completed the move back to the convent, there was one more shock in store for me. I was called to Mother Superior's room to be informed of my father's will. I knew nothing of wills, having only come across them in story books where their reading was usually a very solemn occasion. I had also never been in Mother Irma's room before, so I realised that whatever she was going to disclose must be quite important. There was only one chair in the room, a straight hard-backed chair without arms, and she indicated I was to sit on it. Remaining standing herself, she picked up a sheet of paper from which she started to read. I found it difficult to concentrate on what was being said to me. My gaze wandered curiously around the room, taking in a washbasin and jug on a table, a prie-dieu on which was a large gold-edged missal, a writing desk and a bed with mosquito posts and netting, a chest of drawers and one or two bits of matting.

Suddenly my ears caught the words ' . . . my wife Nang Mat and her two children . . . ' which made me leap up shouting, 'That's a mistake. That's not true. That's not my mother. My mother was Khin Nyun.' But Mother Irma pressed on reading that I, then twelve years old, was to remain in the care of the nuns until reaching the age of twenty-one, with the provision of a hundred pounds a year. But I heard no more, for the shock of hearing the words 'my wife Nang Mat' must have shut down my memory at that point, and I cannot remember what was said after those words. I had tried to force Mother Irma into admitting that there had been a mistake in my mother's name but she would not stop. As she read on, she reminded me of Father Boldrini at burial services, aware of the grief of the bereaved, but carrying on with the ritual of the burial liturgy and performing his duty. In the same way Mother Irma seemed to look at me with pity in her eyes, while carrying out her sad duty, her voice droning on like Father Boldrini's quite unaware that I was not hearing a word.

After she finished speaking, she let me give way to uncontrollable sobs as, thoroughly shaken, I clung to the bedpost for support. Nor did she try to restrain me as disbelief mingled with a sense of betrayal and deceit, hatred of my father and Nang Mat, whoever she was, and the total helplessness of my situation bore down on me. So Sister Christine was right after all – I was going to be a charity child and unlike the other children. Gradually a stunned calm settled on me and with it also the realisation that I was now totally dependent on the convent.

The memory of that day has never quite left me, and the feeling of desertion and betrayal of both my mother and myself clung for a very long time. Trying to come to terms with all I had just heard, I made my mind go back to scenes I remembered as far back as the last days in Loilem in order to try and find some reason for my mother's sadness, my father's sternness and never seeing my parents together again after being left at school. Never having heard of divorce or separation, except through death, I found it hard to believe that my father would abandon my mother for someone else, and for this I now hated him. Reluctantly, I had to admit that it all began to add up and now I saw quite clearly why life had changed so much after leaving Loilem. Was that why the nuns seemed to have treated my mother as a nobody? Did they know all the time? Was that why my mother had to take a job packing cheroots into bundles? Was that also why mother seemed to lose face in the village of Sat-thwa, keeping herself more and more to herself? I decided my father must have been a hard cruel man to inflict so much unhappiness on my mother, and he could not have cared for me either, although that was a less bitter pill to swallow.

Realisation of all this now altered my attitude to the nuns. I could see how much I was thrown upon their mercy. A hundred pounds sounded a lot of money to me, but I didn't know about such things. Suppose it wasn't enough? The look on Mother Superior's face implied it was not. I was still a charity child. So would this mean they could force me into becoming a nun? They were always praying for vocations. But at the same time I did not want to be sent away. They were the only world I knew. It was quite clear what I had to do. I would show my gratitude by making myself so useful that they would never tell me to go away.

The convent was ready at last and the longed for return took place. To show how much they appreciated their considerable help the nuns gave the soldiers the use of the larger classrooms to hold parties and dance to gramophone records in the evenings. The girls the soldiers brought to these parties were from the WAAF and they looked just like Marie Burjorgee (who, incidentally, had left school as there was nothing the nuns could do for her). They were emphatically made-up and totally uninhibited in their behaviour and speech. Wide-eyed, we hung over the banisters taking in all we could see, the way they danced, swinging their hips in a manner we knew the nuns would call provocative, close and intimate in all their movements and so daring, almost brazen. It was not long before we were caught, given a sound scolding and dispatched to our dormitories. Next time the soldiers arrived for a party it was to be met at the entrance by a blackboard on which they were severely warned about the unsuitability of their language, their dancing and their behaviour in general. Dancing was to be done in a modest and decorous manner and there was to be no coarse laughter.

New pupils flocked to the school and among them I was overjoyed to recognise girls from pre-war days. There was kind Rosie Verma who had befriended me in that fairyland of her own devising when I was very small and very lonely, and her clever sister Lillie, both still with their long dark Indian plaits. The new girls seemed so exciting, grown-up and sophisticated. They had such lovely dresses and a great deal to tell. Some had news of former pupils who had perished with their parents on the trek to India, the fate of so many who had fled the Japanese, only to meet worse dangers en route. This news made us very sad. But as friendships were renewed we also heard of those who had survived.

There was Peggy West, for instance, who kept us transfixed with her story of her family's escape to India, the three young daughters dressed in shorts with boyish haircuts to avoid undesirable attention, and precious stones sewn into their underwear to buy their way out of trouble, should the need arise. Would I have proved as much of a heroine as Peggy who, aged twelve, was the one who memorised her father's instructions accurately and kept her mother and small brother and sisters going by steamer up the hazardous Hooghly and then by various Indian trains to the Loretto convent in Saugor? At each refugee camp along the way new arrivals would write their names and hoped-for destination on blackboards, and that was how Mr West was at last reunited with his family.

Among the new intake was a girl called Mary Saw, whose father U Saw was to play a major role in the assassination of Aung San, father of Burma's charismatic leader, Aung San Suu Kyi, in 1947, and for this dark deed, was hanged. The Shan girls also returned. Most of them were the daughters of *sawbwas* and still considered to be very rich. There were now about thirty boarders and the nuns needed all the help they could find. Soon I had an opportunity to keep my resolve that I would make myself useful. Parents were keen to make up for the lost years of schooling, and optional extra music featured largely. So it became my job to help the little ones who took piano lessons with their practice, and patiently I took them through the scales, arpeggios and five-finger exercises they were set, over and over again.

Mother Irma had been observing me closely and now put another proposition to me. She would place me in charge of about eight little girls in a dormitory of my own. I would be in sole charge of them, responsible for everything except lessons. My duties were to get them up in the morning, help them dress, make sure they were clean and tidy, their shoes shining, clothes in a good state of repair, in time for Mass, and get them off to bed at night. The eldest children in the group were about seven, but the others were four or five, the age I had been when first entering the convent in 1938. I welcomed the challenge and was thrilled that so much trust had been placed in me, confident that I could justify it.

At first it seemed easy. I was eager to prove myself and all went well. Seeing my little charges spruce and tidy, in time for Mass, putting them to bed at the end of the day, washed and brushed, filled me with a sense of achievement and satisfaction. But waking up the smallest ones to use their potties in the night to prevent accidents was exhausting, and an epidemic of head lice forced on me the unpleasant job of having to douse their heads in kerosene oil, listening all the while to their howls of misery. As most of them were totally unable to dress them-selves in English clothes and were quite unused to putting on ties and lacing up shoes, it all had to be done for them. Making their beds and putting up their mosquito nets also took up a great deal of time. Especially those mosquito nets which were, of course, worth their weight in gold and had to be treated care-fully. During the week I was allowed to scoop them up at the hem and sling them over the top of the bedposts. But Sunday was different. It required the ends to be tucked precisely under the mattress so that the blue bands by which they were tied in made a symmetrical row down the length of the dormitory for the nuns' inspection.

Alongside all this my school work was not to suffer nor was helping pupils with piano practice to stop. It was soon obvious to anyone who could see, that it was too much to expect of one twelve-year-old and, without being made to feel a failure, I was relieved of my unrealistic duties and allowed back with my own age group and friends.

Another idea occurred to Mother Superior which was also doomed to failure. It was that I should take on the task of playing the harmonium in the chapel, and the organ in church, relieving Sister Antonietta for more communal devotions. I was so anxious to succeed at this after the failure of the dormitory-minding scheme that I was overcome by nerves and my fingers shook with such panic that it was a mystery how they ever struck the right notes. Mother Superior was very cross indeed and this time did make me feel that I had incurred her severe displeasure.

At last Lucy and Mary had news of their father and their little brother John who were both safe and well and would be reunited with them one day when all would be revealed about their plight during the Japanese occupation. It was wonderful news for them, and they were thrilled and excited. The nuns were asked to fit them out with anything they needed and they were kind enough to insist that I also share in their good fortune when new dresses were made for them.

I was very touched that they wanted me to be dressed exactly like them, hoping that we would pass off as sisters. But a rather pressing need remained, one that I was not able to voice either to the nuns or even to Lucy or Mary, and that was the problem of underwear. Some of the new girls wore just the same sort of bodice that my mother used to wear under her transparent *eingyi*. These bodices were finely pleated with beautiful lacework and supported by the thinnest of straps; I had heard the *phongyis* berating the women for the immodesty of them. Some of the Anglo-Indian and European girls, however, wore brassières which had a great number of straps and seemed to me very complicated to put on. I felt that I also needed to wear something like a bodice or a brassière, but I was too afraid to ask the nuns to supply me with one. I thought long and hard and came up with a solution. On Sunday mornings we were allowed to get up half an hour later than usual, so I chose that time to steal into the cupboards where the dirty clothes were collected in baskets. Quickly I sorted through them, not enjoying the stale smell, but eventually finding something that fitted. I felt so much more comfortable that I repeated this performance every Sunday, learning to put up with the stale unfresh brassière or bodice.

Now at last we discovered that Lucy was actually fifteen years old and Mary, at thirteen, was one year older than me. I wasn't the one in the middle after all. I was with the Greys until 1947 and during all that time I never met their father, or their little brother John, and I began to wonder whether the father would ever show up. But theirs was a complicated story, the details of which I only learnt much later. Mr Grey had remarried in India during the war an English lady who did not want to have anything to do with half-Burmese daughters of his first marriage nor, by Mary's account, did she want her husband to have any contact with them either. I have a long letter from Lucy and Mary written on 30 July 1948. It was full of news about how the school was progressing, and how they were spending their Easter holidays with 'our Aunty Margaret and our brother Johnny. We enjoyed ourselves thoroughly going to Maymyo and Mandalay', but there was no mention of their father. Lucy, on leaving school in Kalaw, went to Rangoon to become a nurse, but because the new Mrs Grey would not have the girls under her roof, she had to stay elsewhere and could only meet her father at pre-arranged places and times. Mary recounts with bitterness that when their father eventually died in Devon she and Lucy were not told of his death for two years.

CHAPTER

|✳✳| **14** |✳✳|

I DISCOVER MY FAMILY

THE SCHOOL WAS NOW really thriving and its reputation spread far and wide. We had all missed a great deal of schooling and there was a sense of urgency to catch up on all that we had missed.

In the rainy season of 1946 a Mr Wright called at the convent asking the nuns if he could see me. He had been the friend of my father with whom we had spent a night on the way to Taunggyi. I remember him as having a very kind wife, and that enormous dog called Caesar. Now he was here with two beautiful little flaxen-haired girls, aged about four and two, and wondered if the nuns would be so kind as to keep them at the school as boarders. They *were* a bit young but arrangements were made to accept them soon.

In the meantime Mr Wright had a piece of information to give regarding my father. Apparently, before the Japanese invasion he had bought a hundred acres of land which had been intended for me, but which Mr Wright was sure would not have been mentioned in the will. Would the nuns give him permission to drive me to the place to show me where it was? Before that piece of news had time to sink in he produced a picture of a small boy dressed in dungarees sitting on a wicker seat, and placed it in my hand. Turning it over I saw written in my father's hand 'John Michael Rossiter, aged 2'. He was a beautiful little round-faced boy with rather slanted eyes, like a Shan's, and quite irresistible, and also like a Shan, quite fair-skinned. I just did not know what to think, so confusing did I find Mr Wright's arrival. For this little boy would be my little half-brother and his mother would have been the woman who took my mother's place with my father. I returned the photograph to Mr Wright because I wanted nothing to do with that woman and her children. Looking back from this great distance I can still recall how very upset I was on behalf of my mother remembering how she had been abandoned. But good manners forced me to thank him for the photograph which he insisted I keep. After all, it was possible that Mr Wright did not know that the little boy's mother and mine were two different women, but at the age of thirteen I was not able to put these questions to him, an adult.

Mother Superior gave permission for him to take me off in his car, leaving his little daughters with the nuns. The land was some miles away. I cannot remember what conversation took place on the drive, as my mind was still in a turmoil over the photograph and all that it implied, and I was too shy to ask any questions. The land, high up on a plateau and totally devoid of any dwellings, was beautiful and in the distance Mr Wright pointed out the famous Lake Inle. The ground was criss-crossed with tiny irrigation streams which made a delicate tinkling sound as they flowed busily to join up with each other. I did not know what to make of this discovery: what was I supposed to do with this land, what did ownership of it mean? It was easy to see that Mr Wright was thinking what an odd child I was, showing neither excitement nor having any questions to ask, but the sensation of actually owning anything was strange, unfamiliar and unsettling.

A most unexpected turn of events came about not long after the visit to see the land. A bundle of letters, torn, soiled and addressed to me via the Japanese Red Cross was put into my hands, years out of date. I had not received a single letter from anybody since the Japanese invasion, so this was a very exciting event. My father used to write before he came to see me on his annual trips; my mother never wrote to me because, although she could of course read and write in Burmese, I would not have been able to read and write in that language, even though I spoke it fluently. Letters were always censored by the nuns, both incoming and outgoing, but these had somehow bypassed the system. The girl to whom this batch had been handed by the postman passed them on to me, seeing my name on the envelopes. There were half a dozen in all, some so damaged as to be already open, written on flimsy air mail paper, in a heavy hand, and they had come from Eire.

My heart pounding, I opened the first of them with unsteady hands. It seemed that a total stranger was writing letters to me, all asking the same questions. 'Where are you? Do you have any news of your mother? Let us know where you are', and more in that vein. Written in 1943 and 1944 (it was now 1946) they had lain in some letter box until this day. Every one was signed 'Your affectionate grandmother'. There was one letter in which she mentioned that 'your sister Patricia is coming home for the holidays' and that she had a cousin coming to stay with her. In one or two letters she wrote that my father had reached India after a most arduous trek, but that he did not have any news of me. My head reeled with all these revelations and my heart was fit to burst with the excitement and the wonder of the news. I had never known that I had a sister, a grandmother or cousin, but now it was all there written in letters, so it must be true. How marvellous to know that I was just like everybody else with a family of my very own. Just as before, when my friends sympathised with me over the loss of my parents, they now shared in my joy and excitement and quickly spread the news to the nuns.

It was unbelievable! Two more bundles of letters arrived soon after the first, one of them containing my very first letter from the sister called Patricia. Written when she was twelve (this would be 1943), she pointed out in big-sisterly fashion that I would now have two figures on my age, as I would be ten, then went on to write about little cousin Valerie who was four but who could not really talk properly.

In my excitement I wondered what she was like, what sort of place they lived in and whether they would have me to live with them. I was sure they would, and hardly able to sleep at nights, I built castle after castle in the air imagining what life would be like in the future. With a jolt I remembered the terms of my father's will which stipulated that I should be in the charge of the nuns until I was twenty-one. That day seemed a very long way away as I was then only thirteen. Sister Antonietta was very happy for me but Mother Superior looked thoughtful and said little.

Sister Christine was in her element as, taking over completely the bundle of letters from my newly found family, she decided to conduct my correspondence with them. Her love of the English language brimmed over as, with eyes aglow and the dictionary at her elbow, she composed and re-composed several epistles, until she was satisfied with her efforts. The results were so ornate and sophisticated that their meaning for the most part was lost on me. However all that was required of me was my best handwriting and signature! My grandmother must have been amazed and impressed that one so young and from such a background could write such letters.

Perhaps that was what prompted her to suggest, or more likely demand, that the nuns should teach me another language. It was Sister Erminia who took on the task of giving me private lessons in Italian, but that apparently was not quite what my grandmother wanted! In one letter to me she said that she thought something like French would have been more appropriate, not realising perhaps that the nuns would probably not know French. By now I was beginning to get an idea that they were finding my grandmother a little bit difficult, especially as they had had to inform her that I had been received into the Catholic Church. The Rossiters were and had always been staunch Protestants for generations and my grandmother was not at all pleased; indeed she wrote to the nuns that they had no right to influence me in such an important matter at so tender an age. All this I learned many years later.

One day I was summoned to the presence of an enormously tall man who was introduced to me as Mr Ogden, my father's old friend whom I had met before the occupation in Taunggyi. I was left alone with him in one of the newly built classrooms. He gave me a long look, at my bare feet and plain shapeless dress, and asked me whether I knew why he had come to see me. I had to tell him I did not, and I often wonder what he thought of me then. The impression I had of him was one of infinite kindness and gentleness for, putting his arm around me, eyes brimming with tears, he murmured over and over again, 'So, this is poor Eddie's little girl.'

Dumbfounded at his tears I just stared at him and must have made a most unfavourable impression. He asked whether there was anything I needed immediately, but I could not think of a thing. Then, giving me another reassuring hug, he said that everything would be all right from now on and left.

My emotions were in a whirl of uncertainty and my mind full of what he could possibly mean, but my convent-training still had its stranglehold on my ability to ask intelligent questions. We children still never queried any decisions taken on our behalf, just accepted whatever was ordained by the nuns to be for our good. That was the way things were. Mary and I have often talked about this since and wished we had asked more questions, perhaps even rebelled a bit at not being told things that were very important to us at the time and for our future. But that would have been seen as extremely brazen. Besides we were completely dependent on the nuns for everything. It was also not seemly to have any desires and wishes of our own and, as I mentioned earlier, we were brought up more like little nuns than normal children.

The more I think of it, the more I am convinced that Mother Irma knew that I had a grandmother and a sister long before I did, for she had a copy of the will in her possession. Surely they would have been mentioned in that. But of course I had not been paying attention in the great upheaval of emotion I was going through at its reading. Maybe at the time she thought that there was never going to be any chance of my joining my new family, and had not my father's will assigned me to the convent until I came of age? She may have thought that it would only complicate matters if I knew that I had a family so many thousand miles away. In the same way Lucy and Mary Grey must also have wondered why it took their father so long to get in touch with them and then, having done so, allowed such a long time to pass before he actually came to see them. Perhaps again Mother Superior had knowledge of these facts all along but decided that it was not in our best interests to pass on the news to us.

Now, as result of Mr Ogden's visit, the unbelievable was happening and Mother Irma told me that I was to join my sister and grandmother in Ireland. This was the most wonderful news I had received in my entire life, because it meant something most important. It meant that I was a person belonging to a family, with an identity of my own. I was no longer a charity child.

When I thought of Mr Ogden's visit I also remembered his beautiful wife and their little girl Elizabeth with the enormous bows, too short tunic and the frilly knickers which had so scandalised the nuns. As the invasion threatened, I learnt afterwards, Mr Ogden had sent his wife and children to safety in India by way of China and had later escaped on foot himself, arriving eventually in Calcutta where he met up with my father. Maybe he had been with him when he died? Maybe he had promised a dying man that he would look for and take care of his lost little daughter? But these, of course, were questions I did not know how to frame, so how could I expect any answers? What I do know was that after the liberation Mr Ogden was one of those involved in handing Burma over to the Burmese, but he still found time to seek out a thirteen-year-old girl and sort out her personal affairs for her. Maybe it was Mr Ogden's diplomacy which saw to it that my father's will was set aside and I was permitted to leave the convent and go, in peril to my immortal soul, to live with my Protestant family? Or maybe it wasn't that much of a battle? Perhaps Mr Ogden's arrival on the scene just made it easier for Mother Superior to part with one pupil she had had under her care long enough.

My only fear now was that something would happen to prevent my departure. Other letters started to arrive and it was with delight that I discovered that there were two aunts in Ireland, both widowed. Aunt Anne had a son Patrick, three years older than me, the other, Aunty Con, having two daughters a bit younger than me. My father had been the eldest of five children. The youngest son, with six children, lived in England, while one other daughter, Frances, lived in Canada. Aunty Con sent me a postcard which showed a happy family group in the country. In it was a groom leading a horse on which sat a boy, while other children walked with the groom. She sent it, she said, because it reminded her of country walks they used to take, with my father riding a horse. Family photographs sometimes came with the letters. In one Patricia, my sister, aged about ten and with pigtails, was riding a donkey on a beach, a young man on either side. I felt a certain alarm as I was afraid I too would have to ride and I was terrified of horses. But these and other letters and pictures painted such a lovely view of life in Ireland that I wanted to get there more than anything else in the world. And I dreamt about how it would be in my new home with my grandmother perhaps telling me about my father when he was young, going to school with my sister, making new friends, picturing it to be anything but what it eventually turned out to be.

It was therefore with the greatest alarm that one day I received the news from one of my companions that a Burman had walked into the playground saying that he was my Uncle U Tun Shein. He very much wanted to see me and had come to take me back to my mother's village. Panic seized me, for I thought he could *make* me go back with him. Seeing my predicament, my friends hid me while they went to fetch Mother Superior who explained to him that as my legal guardians they had made plans to let me go to my father's family in Ireland.

Once the village of Sat-thwa had encompassed my idea of earthly bliss, but I, like Lucy and Mary, had been educated away from our Burmese roots by fathers ambitious to do the best for us by making us more like themselves. If my mother had still been alive wild Irish horses would not have removed me from Burma. But she was not, and it was four years since I had seen any of her family. So to my eternal shame my poor uncle was forced to leave without seeing me and I was filled with remorse for having behaved so shabbily towards him.

CHAPTER

|✳|✳| 15 |✳|✳|

OUT INTO THE WIDE WORLD

PREPARATION NOW BEGAN in earnest for my departure. This involved making new dresses, according to the ability of the nuns and the availability of dress patterns. For the first time in four years shoes had to be considered, but as there were no shoe shops they had to be made to measure by the local Indian shoe-maker. They were ill-fitting and agony to walk in. However I would have to get used to them, although the gym shoes given us by the Red Cross recently were more comfortable and I had made up my mind to get rid of the leather shoes at the first opportunity.

Still overwhelmed with anxiety that something would happen to prevent me leaving the school, I found sleep difficult and was plagued by bad dreams. In these trains were derailed or overtaken by dacoits or both, the nuns would not let me go, or my mother's people lay in wait to take me away by force, which is apparently what nearly happened to Lucy and Mary when their mother died. To add to the tension, a mysterious packet of newspapers arrived addressed to me, containing news of the bombing of Nagasaki and Hiroshima. I saw that the sender was a Mr Livesey, whose name was vaguely familiar from my visits to Taunggyi, but I could not remember him at all and there was no explanatory letter. We had, of course, heard of the dreadful atom bombs but that was some time ago. It was all very odd and no one knew what to make of it.

Almost every day the nuns entreated me with great earnestness to remember that I was a Catholic and that I must not be persuaded to become a Protestant, that I should insist on going to a Catholic school in Ireland, and pray for the conversion of my grandmother and sister. Reverend Mother gave dire warnings of the dangers that lay lurking ahead in the great big world, and that I was to be on constant guard against them. She never hinted what these dangers were, but the frequency with which she warned of them only made me anticipate them with secret delight. In my already overflowing mind she had given me a new problem to wrestle with, but to all her admonitions I could only give a firm promise to be a good girl, as often as she required it.

Two dates were set for my departure, only to be postponed. On both occasions the trains had been derailed by dacoits, just as in my dreams, and I now really believed I would never get away. My fears were groundless, as on the third set date an Indian man arrived to escort me by train to Rangoon. I had been ready for days, trying to hide my excitement, promising to write to everybody, promising not to forget anybody. Yet was I nervous, I wonder, that morning, just the smallest bit reluctant to leave the convent and familiar faces with whom I had lived through so much? Strange now to look back and see them so clearly before me, the people who made me and moulded me and are, in part, responsible for whatever I am today.

Lucy and Mary had not yet seen their father. He was working in Rangoon, probably still with Steel Brothers, and my heart went out to them, waiting so patiently for their great day to come. It was time to go. My companions gathered in the compound to wish me good-bye, even Aridiem Mary and Teresina, old Joseph and Josephine, my godmother. There were no presents to exchange but I knew that a great deal of well wishing went with me, together with their prayers.

Now Mother Superior took me aside and, stooping low, she hung a little cloth bag around my neck. 'Look after it well,' she said in a voice unsteady with emotion. 'It's all we have but you might need it, so keep it safe and hidden under your blouse. There's a hundred rupees there for the journey. Be a good girl, don't forget us, and don't forget your prayers.'

For the first time the full realisation of what I owed these nuns affected me. I had been so full of excitement that I had hardly given any time to think of all they had done for me for all those years. But my Indian escort was getting impatient and we had a train to catch. How different my last train journey had been, I could not help remembering, for then I had been with my mother coming back from Sat-thwa, not realising I would never see her or the village again. My Indian escort and I had the carriage to ourselves and I looked out first on one side, then on the other. Imagine my surprise when at a spot near the stream where we had picked raspberries and collected beetles long ago, the children had gathered together for one last farewell, and were waving their handkerchieves to me. I shed tears then at the loss of my known world and all who inhabited it. The Indian patted me on the head and said words of comfort.

That night we stopped at Thazi, as it was definitely not safe for trains to travel at night. Standing on the platform was one of the big girls who had been at the school in Kalaw, and when she saw me she obtained permission from my escort to take me to her house to spend the night. This was the first night that I had ever spent away from the school for years, and it was a strange and unsettling feeling. So strange not to have any rules to obey, to be living outside the convent, to be asked what I would like to eat or where I wanted to sit or when I would like to go to bed. What a lot of unusual sensations I was beginning to experience.

Next morning we continued on our journey by train. This time there seemed to be a lot of British soldiers travelling on it, and one or two of them spoke to me. Again what a strange sensation, being spoken to by a man who was not Father Boldrini without the nuns' permission. They were on their way to Rangoon to return to England on the next troopship. I had no idea how my passage had been arranged, but they seemed to think we would meet on board. Even that word troopship had an odd ring to it. Certainly it was not a term I had heard before.

It must have been about the end of March. The further we got away from Kalaw the hotter it became and by the time we reached Rangoon I had become very uncomfortable with the unaccustomed heat. Dazed by all the unusual happenings in the past few weeks, together with the heat and the upheaval of my departure from school, for the first time I had the odd sensation that the real me was standing and watching someone else go through the motions of every day life, that the real me had no part in all this. My Indian escort took me to a chauffeur-driven car, together with my one suitcase containing everything

I owned in the world. The drive was bewildering, as we veered round enormous bomb craters, the traffic barely avoiding pedestrians and drivers keeping their hands pressed on the horn. At last we came to a halt outside a big office building and I was ushered into Mr Ogden's presence. Mr Ogden was glad to see me arrive safely and welcomed me with open arms. Looking me over, he could barely conceal a gentle smile of amusement at the dress I was wearing which seemed so quaint to him. This made me fight back my tears for I was now beginning to feel pangs of homesickness for the nuns and my friends. However it soon passed in the talk of arranging a passport and also a ration book and coupons for use in Ireland. I had no idea what that was all about, but Mr Ogden's secretary Marlene said she would see to it all. I almost did not recognise Marlene. She had been the head girl at St Agnes's when I first went there, and her sister Vera was in the same class as me. I was just as awestruck by Marlene now as I had been all those years ago. Marlene also undertook to help find me something more suitable to wear. I told Mr Ogden that Reverend Mother had given me a hundred rupees and that I could buy things for myself, but he only smiled, shaking his head, and saying gently that a hundred rupees would not go very far.

It was the end of the business day and time to go home. In the car the sense of unreality gripped me once again, but then something totally out of my experience happened. When the car turned left or right an amber indicator shot out with a click, giving the direction it was turning. This had a profound effect on me. For I reasoned that if so small a matter had been considered important enough to deserve such detail of attention, surely it also meant that everything from now on was indeed going to be all right? This was going to be the start of what Mr

Ogden had promised when he saw me in Kalaw – that 'everything would be all right'. It was as though some force was giving reassurance that where there had been total darkness before, with just one switch of the hand, everything would be all right once more.

|✳|✳| 16 |✳|✳|

MR OGDEN'S RANGOON

MR OGDEN HAD A SUITE of rooms in a large block called, I think, Government Buildings. Marlene also had a room here and I had another, a huge room all to myself. Although I was quite exhausted by the end of the first evening, I saw there was a washbasin with taps in the room and, because I had not seen such a thing for years, I simply had to try turning the taps on and off, just to see if they worked. Sleep did not come easily that night, for the events of the day had been too exciting. Two other things kept me awake, first the prickly heat which covered me from head to foot and second the fear of sleeping on my own in such a large room. I tried turning on the fan over my bed, but it made such a whirring sound that it kept me awake.

Early next morning a cup of tea was brought to me by an Indian servant. When I dressed I put on my school uniform as it seemed a safer option than the new dress everyone found so quaint. Then, not knowing what to do with myself next, I made my way to Mr Ogden's room, quite unannounced. Wearing only a towel around his middle he stood in front of a mirror shaving. I hardly noticed that he was undressed, so spellbound was I by the sound of beautiful music.

'Where is that lovely music coming from?' I asked. He pointed to a radio in a corner. 'Are people really playing music so early in the morning?' I said, for it was only about six o'clock.

His answer did not come immediately, for he paused just a moment and a faraway look came into his eyes, as though he saw a memory from a long way back; perhaps he was seeing my father in Calcutta, or perhaps he was wondering what was going to become of me. Smiling kindly, he said, 'What a lot you're going to have to learn! No, people don't get up that early as a rule to play music, it's a recording, and another thing, you should really knock on a bedroom door before you enter.' This was said so gently that I was not made to feel lacking in good manners. Then we went down to breakfast.

In an enormous room scores of tables had been laid with immaculately starched white tablecloths with Burmese and Indian waiters in attendance. I remembered we used to have such waiters in school before the war. And now came my first experience of British food, fruit juice, cereal, bacon and eggs, followed by toast and marmalade – such a feast as I had never seen. We were joined by Marlene, and all around people were nodding their heads in greeting with a questioning glance or two in my direction. For I was still oddly dressed for such a place in my navy gym slip, white blouse and gym shoes.

Another day I put on the debatable dress and the Indian chauffeur was instructed to drive me to have a passport photograph taken. Recently I came across this. It shows a girl with a long face like a peanut, dark shoulder-length hair held back with hair clips, very dark rings under her eyes and something in her expression to suggest that she had been heavily drugged, so dejectedly tired and confused did she look. That done, when Marlene had spare time, she took me to buy some clothes. She was unsure what to get and we ended up with something I could wear in Ireland, a Gor-ray skirt in a rust colour, and a green short-sleeved jumper. It was so unusual to be asked whether I would like this garment rather than another that I think Marlene became a bit impatient at what she took to be my lack of enthusiasm and interest. She also bought me a bathing costume to wear on the boat in case it had a swimming pool. Our excursion had not been a success and barely able to disguise her exasperation, she was glad when it was over.

I had no idea how long I would be spending in Rangoon, neither did Mr Ogden as my passage had not been fixed. During the day I amused myself sometimes by walking around with an Indian servant in attendance, visiting bazaars and shops, but I was not on my own very often. Those were wonderful days with Mr Ogden in Rangoon. I could go in and out of his room as I pleased, touch and look at everything around me. And there was a lot to see. Especially attractive was the beautifully carved set of wooden figures representing the different tribes of the Shan States in their distinctive costumes. Following an elder sister, he also took a serious interest in homeopathy, and one whole wall was lined with hundreds of phials of tiny identical white pills. On his desk was something fascinating like a small black box with a strip of light-coloured smooth rubbery material set in it which he would massage gently with his sensitive fingers, concentrating hard until suddenly the rubbing fingers made a noticeably different sound, and a light came into his eyes, as if he had discovered what he was looking for. I learnt later it was some sort of radionic diagnostic instrument made by De La Warr, which operated on the dowsing principle. He sometimes gave me a few of the pills from various bottles, but they all tasted the same, and I wondered how he could tell them apart. This hobby later became his living, for he became a homeopath and radionic practitioner in Dublin some years later.

I must in my own way have been quite a puzzle to him. Sometimes he had a wonderful way of showing he was amused by something I had said or done. 'Blight, smut and mildew!' he would boom. 'What do we have here?' Or feigning exaggerated interest, 'Is *that* what the good nuns told you? Good gracious me!' Sometimes even, with amused mockery in his voice, 'What *would* the good nuns say about this?' He found it amazing that my head was so full of religion, especially sin and punishment. 'Good Lord, what *have* the good nuns filled your mind with?' Once I stopped dead in my tracks as twelve o'clock struck to say the Angelus, just as we used to do in the convent. He did not exactly stop me doing this, but somehow I got the impression that people in his circle were not accustomed to praying in public.

This was my first taste of life outside the convent, and I stood goggle-eyed as scene after scene presented itself before my eyes. In the dining room every evening there were beautiful women in elegant gowns, for the most part low-cut or backless. I'm afraid I did stare quite hard at their dresses, for I had never seen anything like them and knew that the nuns would disapprove of them all. And then there was the dancing, more elegant than that of the soldiers and the WAAFs, but still noticeably intimate and what the nuns would term 'immodest'.

We must have presented rather an incongruous picture as we entered the dining room every night, he very tall, extremely handsome and distinguished, immaculate in his dinner jacket, while I, still wearing my school uniform and plimsolls (the Gorray skirt was strictly for Ireland) would be hanging on to his arm, awkwardly because of the immense difference in our heights.

Unsophisticated as I was, I could yet sense that a lot of the ladies would have loved to be in my position because they made a great fuss of me, hoping to draw his attention to themselves. He never appeared embarrassed escorting such a raw, uncouth girl but took my arm with much gallantry, making me feel almost their equal. He loved talking to me about his daughter Elizabeth, a year younger than me and whom he promised I would meet again one day. He was immensely proud of her and showed her photograph to everyone, insisting that they saw a likeness between her and the royal princesses Elizabeth and Margaret Rose.

Mr Ogden took me everywhere he went in the evenings, quite undeterred by the suitability or otherwise of the occasion. We went to cocktail parties, soirées, government receptions, concerts, formal dinner parties, the cinema, and private supper parties at the houses of friends, for he had a wide and sophisticated circle. The first film I ever saw was *Frenchman's Creek*. I loved the lavish scenery, the costumes and colour, the glamorous stars and music, but did not understand the real implication of the plot, for my English was not up to it, and when in the end the heroine did not run away with the Frenchman I was inconsolable. I can hear Mr Ogden's voice now saying, 'What, and you a good Catholic girl? You wouldn't have her leave her husband and children to go away with that French pirate, would you? What would the holy nuns say if they could hear you?' and he laughed uproariously.

Sometimes, dismissing the chauffeur and driving the car himself, he would burst into song. His was a beautiful voice, full and rich, and although in fun he made me the focus of his songs I was never embarrassed, for it was the voice that completely won me over. The only other male voice I had heard was Father Boldrini's at Mass as he intoned the Gloria in Excelsis and the Credo. His was a rich Italian voice, also beautifully in tune, but of course I had never heard him sing the sort of songs that Mr Ogden sang. Finding that I loved to listen to him singing, he was delighted to learn that the nuns had taught me to play the piano and he sang whenever possible, just to please me.

I loved these drives with him without the chauffeur. At the Burmese New Year there is a water festival (*Thin Gyan*), just before the monsoon starts, when it is the custom for people to pour buckets of water over each other. Sometimes scented water is used on ladies, but the more rumbustious use hose-pipes from the top of open trucks to give vent to their high spirits. At least the Burmese only use plain water, unlike the Indians celebrating *holi* with all the colours of the palette. One day, as we stopped at the traffic lights during the festive period, our car door was wrenched open and we got the full force of a bucket of water thrown over us both. Mr Ogden only laughed good naturedly and waved to the people, even though we had to turn round and return to his rooms to change into dry clothes.

It was amazing how quickly I adapted to this new life and it was with a delicious anticipation that I awoke each morning wondering what new excitement the day would bring. One Burmese family were so kind as to give me some precious gems to have set into a ring. One jolly Englishman gave me a deck chair to take on board the troopship, for he assured me that there were never enough to go round. Quite what I was to expect on this ship I was not sure, but it all added to my keen sense of anticipation.

The day arrived when a passage was fixed for me on board the SS *Cheshire*, leaving at the beginning of April. This was now 1947 and a few days before my fourteenth birthday which I would be spending on board. There was some difficulty about finding someone who would keep a kindly eye on me during the three-week long voyage, but Mr Ogden was confident of finding someone on the quayside and on the day of departure he scanned the faces of my fellow passengers for a likely candidate. The lady he settled on was a Mrs Mitchell whose husband he had known in the Burma Frontier Service. I was introduced and she kindly agreed to keep an eye on me, as we shared a cabin with two other ladies.

It was time for Mr Ogden to go, as Mrs Mitchell was waiting for me to accompany her up the gangway. Tearful and forlorn I said good-bye to him, unable to let him know how much I had loved him for all the kindness he had shown me over the last three weeks and how full my heart was with gratitude for all he had done. He had opened up such a new world to me, a world of glamour, fun and excitement. But he told me not to be sad, for his wife would be meeting me at Liverpool and we would all meet up again some day.

It did not take long to settle myself in the cabin with the other three ladies. My belongings took very little time to unpack for I had only the one suitcase and my deck chair. Mrs Mitchell was a motherly soul and did not put too many restrictions on me, so that as soon as I had unpacked I ran up on deck to watch the hundreds of passengers still climbing up the gangway. Further down the ship could be seen an orderly stream of soldiers and I wondered if the ones I had met at Thazi on the train would also be embarking. I watched all manner of little craft weaving in and out as they tried to sell their merchandise, holding up their wares for the embarking passengers to see. My excitement was now at fever pitch, I had never been so free to do as I wished before, and the newly found freedom was exhilarating.

CHAPTER

|❋|❋| 17 |❋|❋|

GOING HOME

WE SET OFF at mid-day down the Rangoon river, enormously wide and muddy, the opposite shore barely visible. Sampans went about their way sometimes perilously close to the big ships, and it was with some impatience that I waited for my first ever sight of the sea. At nightfall I was obliged to give up, for we had still not reached it, but early in the morning there it was, grey-green and vast. Very soon I did as the other passengers, walking round and round the decks and getting to know some of them. I discovered that one of the lower decks was full of British soldiers, and I even caught sight of the one or two I had met on the train from Kalaw. They were restricted to their quarters but every now and then we waved to each other.

Three days later we reached Colombo. I wondered if we would be allowed ashore and, if so, whether Mrs Mitchell would let me accompany her and her friends. But she had assumed I would be joining them and we made for the Palm Beach Hotel. It was my first experience of being on a beach, and this one was white sand, ringed with palm trees. Unable to swim, I nevertheless enjoyed sitting in my new bathing costume, watching the agile native boys climbing the trees to hurl down coconuts, while people swam and sported in the water.

We were not allowed ashore at Aden, our next port of call, but the arrival of all sorts of small junk boats with their colourful array of goods for sale went some way to make up for the disappointment. The haggling was noisy and the more dauntless shinned their way up the side of the ship on rope ladders. It was with difficulty that the crew managed to get them off just before we left port.

Next we entered the Red Sea and, after a couple of days, the Suez Canal. It was unbearably hot and humid but the realisation came to me that right now I was actually experiencing all the places and people I had been learning about in my geography books. Imagine being in the Suez Canal, I thought. Nothing had prepared me for this, the wonderful feeling that I could almost touch both sides of the canal, and watching the camels with their riders, so like the pictures in the Old Testament. The heat and humidity brought on my prickly heat again, but everyone kept telling me that the Mediterranean would be much cooler, which it was. Once we left Aden we did not stop at all and any land we could see from the ship was too distant to make out landmarks. The Bay of Biscay was incredibly rough and the decks emptied. I was surprised by this at first, until I too succumbed to seasickness.

It was during this part of the journey that an old man called Mr Crowe approached me and, learning that I was travelling on my own, asked if I would let him have my tobacco allowance as he was sure I did not smoke! Not really knowing what he was talking about as I had no experience of duty-free allowances, I agreed, because I had been brought up to be obliging to adults. Conspiratorially, he handed me my cigarette allowance, saying he would reclaim them on our arrival at Liverpool.

We reached Liverpool at mid-morning. Crowds thronged the pier waving and shouting to the people on board. Mrs Mitchell was soon swept up by her friends while I searched the landing area from every deck hoping to catch a glimpse of Mrs Ogden. I thought I would recognise her, although it was quite some time since I had last seen her. The decks were emptying quickly and I had to admit to growing a bit forlorn and apprehensive. But after a worrying hour or so I was relieved to see someone looking equally worried as Mrs Ogden was searching in turn for me. She had hardly changed, was still beautiful, graceful and charming, but was not too pleased that Mr Crowe had asked me to hang on to his cigarettes. We thought we should give him half an hour or so, then still not seeing him, decided that she would post the cigarettes to him, not realising that we did not have his address!

We had some time to spare before catching the plane to Dublin so Mrs Ogden decided that we should go to a shop or two to get me something more suitable to wear to meet my grandmother and sister for the first time. Unlike the shops in Rangoon those in Liverpool were like Aladdin's cave to me, even making allowance for the austere period of rationing and coupons through which England was going. Again I was totally incapable of making a choice when presented with more than one garment, and I would have been only too happy for Mrs Ogden to do that for me, but she, trying to be kind, thought I should be the one to choose. The noise and bustle of the crowds and traffic were alarming but, most disappointing of all, I could hardly understand a word of the kind of English spoken by the Liverpudlians. I did not hear anyone speak like Mr and Mrs Ogden, it sounded almost like a foreign language and they spoke so quickly.

Mrs Ogden then discovered that my passport was not valid for Eire, and after a futile effort trying to get this put right, she gave up and decided that I would just have to try and pass off as her daughter Elizabeth and use her passport. By now I was totally confused and only too glad to board the plane, for the end of the journey was near and I would have to be patient for only a couple of hours more.

I tried my hardest to settle down in my seat and be calm, but when the aeroplane gathered speed on the runway before taking flight it was difficult to keep my resolve. I tried to distract myself by looking out over the Irish Channel and picking out the ships below, wondering if Mrs Ogden sitting beside me could sense my agitation. She had of course given me the window seat. It was a beautiful clear late afternoon at the end of April. In Burma, it would already have been dark. I tried to make myself think of all the nuns and my friends left in Burma and the bits of my life that would live there forever, and of kind Mr Ogden; I pictured the convent, and Lucy and Mary, imagining what they would be doing now, but it was useless. My mind raced in anticipation of my new life which would begin as soon as the plane landed at Collinstown Airport.

At last the plane was descending, and the first thing I saw of Ireland were rabbits hopping about in a vividly green field. Now it was flying so low that in the distance I could see people waving from a balcony. Was my sister one of them and would she recognise me, or I her, from the photographs we had exchanged, I wondered. I wanted to run out down the steps of the plane but, knowing I would have to follow everyone else, I tried to be patient. We walked sedately across the tarmac and in a daze I was taken through the immigration procedures. Suddenly the waiting was all over. We ran to each other, for I had recognised her at once, not by the recently exchanged photographs, but by a picture I had remembered seeing a long, long time ago. She was the little girl in my mother's powder compact.

CHAPTER

|❋|❋| 18 |❋|❋|

GOING BACK

Very many years later, when I was married and had children of my own, my father's sister Aunt Anne asked me quite unexpectedly one day, 'Do you know how you and your sister got your names?' I had to admit that I had never given this a thought but I was eager to hear what she had to say.

'Neither you nor your sister were named when you were born. I know you were called by pet names, Big Baby and Little Baby, but you could hardly class them as proper names. I asked your father over and over again when he was going to get round to giving you both real names, but he always evaded the issue. Perhaps he couldn't be bothered because you weren't boys. So I decided to take matters into my own hands. I bought two silver hair brushes which had 'Patricia' engraved on one and 'Maureen' on the other and had them sent out to Burma. So you two were named after your hair brushes.'

After my arrival in Dublin I had expected to receive answers to all my childhood questions about my parents and their life together. I would also be entering an exciting world I had so far only read about or glimpsed in my grandmother's letters, and I had a childish confidence that there was a place waiting there for me where I would belong. But this was not to be. The tantalising gaps in my family story were not about to be filled in. Burma was not a country to be mentioned in my grandmother's household. She would not even have in the house a copy of Maurice Collis's book *Lord of the Sunset* which was an account of the author's tour of the Shan States in the 1930s on part of which he was accompanied by my father, whose excellent quality photographs are reproduced in the book. So what little I learnt about the past did not come from my grandmother.

My father is long dead now and past all criticism. By all accounts he was very intelligent, fluent in many languages, especially those of the Shan States, but also a bit of a loner. It must be said to his credit at that time that he did marry my mother, when many Europeans did not always legitimise their Burmese or Shan offspring. And there is no record I know of that he ever divorced her. Apart from Mr Ogden, I have not come across anyone who knew him well, certainly no one who could tell me what he was really like. One cosmopolitan Burman who had met him several times had always imagined him to be a bachelor.

The revelation about the hair brushes I could, after the lapse of years, find rather amusing. But the story I pieced together of my mother's early years of married life was less so. That Patricia was the little infant playmate who disappeared when my parents went away was something I had by now worked out. Leaving me behind with one of my mother's sisters in Monywa, my parents had taken her on a long six-months' leave to Ireland.

During this period my mother had to undergo an operation for the removal of her appendix and another more serious one. A hysterectomy is hinted at. How strange and frightening she must have found the experience of hospital, especially as she did not understand any English. Almost worse, some hotels turned her away when they were touring because she was considered coloured – she who when newly married had gloried in the name of Ma Phyu (Miss White) in recognition of the desirable paleness of her skin.

When my parents returned to Burma they left Patricia behind with my grandmother in Ireland. I don't know whether my mother had a say in this arrangement and would hazard a guess that she did not. The picture of the little girl in her compact certainly made her very unhappy and she must have missed her dreadfully. After another of his trips home one of my father's other sisters, Frances, accompanied him back to Burma for a holiday and it was to her that he put forward the proposal that she should adopt me. She wisely declined the suggestion! So if I was not to be brought up in Ireland, I was to be turned into a reasonably acceptable European by the nearest local method to hand and that was how I came to be packed off to St Agnes's.

My poor mother could not have been happy at the thought of her one remaining child being sent away to school so soon after their return from Ireland. Perhaps this was when the marriage finally broke down, for I never saw them together again after leaving Loilem and being placed in school in Kalaw. I am certain that my father gave my mother an allowance to live on which came to an end for whatever reason during the last holiday I spent with her. I am not clear who it was that told me of my father's plans for me to go to Ireland at the end of 1941.

He must have informed the nuns and asked them to have me kitted out with suitable warm clothing. I quite clearly remember old Mother Josephine on the verge of telling me something important during those lonely holidays, then thinking better of it. I wonder what I would have done if I had known what was being planned for me; probably run away again for I could not have entertained the idea of separation from my mother.

Even today I do not know quite why it took so long after the war ended for anyone to discover I was alive and living in the convent with the nuns in Kalaw. Means of communication must have been difficult in Burma. Both Lucy and Mary Grey and I were kept in a state of cruel ignorance, perhaps under the misguided belief that what we didn't know couldn't do us any harm; for I am sure that the nuns knew a great deal more than they told us. I never discovered the identity of the British officer who brought the news of my parents' death to the nuns and eventually to me, nor by what means a copy of my father's will came into the hands of Mother Superior. Mention must have been made in it about his plans for my sister in Ireland, but I admit to having a lapse of memory over the reading of the will, overwhelmed as I had been by the chance discovery of his new liaison. Looking back from this distance to that searing day it is no longer possible for me to judge with any accuracy what actually was said or read out to me by Mother Irma.

One day while searching for a particular letter, I came across one written by my mother's brother U Tun Shein, the uncle who had tried to visit me in the convent shortly before my departure from Burma. Although I had treated him most shabbily then and had been filled with remorse ever since, he wrote to me in Ireland in Burmese, giving news and details of my mother's family. Because I could not read Burmese, I eventually, in the early 'eighties, made contact with a professor at the School of Oriental and African Studies at London University. With her help I was able to attend a class where I could brush up on the language that once was the only one I could speak. I dug out my uncle's letter and took it along. The professor was so impressed by the perfection and simplicity of language in which this letter was written that she asked if she could use it with her students. And that is how a photocopy of it came to be open on the table at a house where the Burmese military attaché in London and his wife were invited for dinner.

Spying my letter on the table, the attaché's wife asked whether she could have a look at her hostess's homework. When she had read it, she said, 'This letter doesn't by any chance belong to someone called Maureen Rossiter, does it?'

The attaché's wife proved to be none other than Rosie Verma. She had come to England on a tour of duty with her husband, and one of the things she was determined to do was to find out what had happened to the little girl she had befriended and whom she remembered seeing left on her own when all the other children had gone home for the holidays; she had even contemplated putting an advertisement in the *Daily Telegraph*. This discovery led to a happy meeting with Rosie and my other old school friend the intrepid Peggy West, now also living in England, and it put me in contact once more with Mary Grey.

Three years ago my youngest daughter, Kathleen, paid a visit to Burma. Of all my five children she looks most like my mother, sometimes heart-stoppingly so, especially on the rare occasions when she wears Burmese clothes. A stay with Mary Grey, now the wife of a retired colonel in the Burmese army was arranged. Both she and Colonel Khin Nyo were wonder-fully kind to Kathleen, looking after her every need. Unknown to me she had gone to Burma armed with a list of my mother's relations hoping to meet some of them, and it was through the kindness of Mary and the colonel that she was able to meet so many.

Her visit caused quite a stir; word had got about of her arrival and wherever she went in Chauk and Taungdwingyi relations crowded in on her. They were obviously very touched and impressed that a young relation had made such an effort to find them, but Kathleen was in no doubt that the people they really wanted to meet were Baby Kyi and Baby Le. In one of the houses she visited in Taungdwingyi she was surprised and delighted to see displayed on the table photographs of my sister Patricia and her family, recently taken. For Patricia had made an attempt to get in touch with them, but somehow it did not get off the ground. They told Kathleen how they remembered my father riding into the village on a horse and seeing my mother in the cheroot factory and some of them parted with precious old photographs of my parents for me. Kathleen made a meticulous list of the relations she met, her most notable discovery being Sein Shan, the first cousin three years older than me who had been my minder in the babies' class. She could remember to this day just what sort of a child I had been, and the fact that she was only allowed to eat when I had finished my meal, and had strict instructions to make sure that I won in all the games we played!

I myself set out for Burma again two months later, hoping to meet some of these relations and perhaps make amends for some of my childhood neglect. Waiting for me on my arrival at Mary and the colonel's house was a much younger cousin, Min Hnit and his young wife, Min Min Aye. It was their intention to take me on a tour of Burma and the Shan States to meet as many relations as possible. They put themselves to great trouble and expense on my behalf and I hope they realised how very much I appreciated their efforts.

At first I tried to work out how I was related to almost everyone who was presented to me; but I was soon in such a daze, as there were so many of them, that I gave up. Very few of them were well off. Sein Shan struggled to make a living by selling pickles in the market. Meeting her again was indeed very moving. At the end of every visit the whole family would assemble to perform *shiko*, the Burmese obeisance which involved prostrating themselves before me on the floor. Alarmed at first, I tried to demur as politely as I could, but it was explained that as I was now an elder of the family it was only right and proper, so I capitulated and accepted it in the spirit in which it was given. Very few of them were able to tell me anything of my mother, or how she died, but they had all heard that she was known either as Ma Hla, meaning Miss Pretty or Ma Phyu, Miss White. To my poor long-suffering childhood companion Sein Shan I tried to make amends by making her a present which she could use advantageously for herself and her five sons. They were all so delighted that I had not totally forgotten the Burmese language.

Very early in the tour we made for Sat-thwa. Even in November it was unbearably hot and the roads extremely bumpy and bone-shattering. The railway station, recognisable only by its Englishness, looked dilapidated and out of place, the road leading to it was almost completely worn away. A vivid, clear-cut picture rose before me of a young Burmese mother leading a child in European school dress fidgeting with the elastic strap of her sun hat, the dust rising up before them as they walked.

We stopped to ask if anyone knew of my mother Khin Nyun's family who had lived there in the late 1930's. Everyone joined in the discussion and eventually a boy was designated to guide us in our car to where the house used to stand. It had suffered a direct hit in one of the bombing raids during the war but my family had luckily not been there at the time. A new house stood in its place and not at all as I remembered our old house to be. Surely the houses did not stand so close to each other in those days? There was an overpowering putrid smell of stagnant pools of water and it was unthinkable that this was the village in which I had spent so many happy holidays with my mother and grandparents. I felt no loss at what I was leaving behind when we left Sat-thwa for it bore no resemblance to the happy place I had remembered it to be.

At long last we reached Kalaw where we were to spend only a night. I would have preferred to be on my own here, to take in at a leisured pace all the places which meant so much to me, to people them with the ghosts of the long lost nuns and playmates so vividly remembered, to hear again their voices and the gentle swishing of the pine trees; I had to make the best of it with my kind relations accompanying me. The convent seemed considerably shrunken and not as awe-inspiring as I had remembered it. Now a state school, some Burmese nuns still retained a part of it and one of them kindly showed me the chapel. It has not changed one bit, except that the clock steadfastly ticking away the minutes was no longer there. I had only to close my eyes to visualise once more the lizards darting across the ceiling, lizards which I used to count over and over again out of complete boredom, waiting to be let out of the chapel.

We visited the church across the road where Father Boldrini

used to reign, now with Father Angelino in his place, and I imagine as much of a challenge to the local authorities as Father Boldrini had been to the Japs. Pictures of Sister Antonietta, Lucy and Mary poured into my mind as I saw in the old register an entry of my Baptism; once again I heard Sister Seraphina's beautiful voice singing the 'Panis Angelicus'.

Next on my list was Salween, the house to which the British had moved us from the convent. Kalaw is now the headquarters of the military and we had to seek their permission to visit the house for it was occupied by the army. I particularly wanted to take a photograph of it, but this was a sensitive operation. The military were adamant that no civilians would be allowed to take pictures; however they were very courteous about it, and I finally persuaded the commanding officer to take the photographs himself as a gesture that I was no agitator and was only there for sentimental reasons.

Silver Oaks, where the Japanese had put us, was rather sad and dilapidated. It was here that I experienced most strongly the pull of the past. Now the residence of a colonel and his family, the retainers readily allowed me to photograph as much as I liked outside and to roam anywhere I wanted as the family were away. The beautiful dignified terraces which had been divided into two by brick steps were now overgrown with weeds. I did not go inside, of course, but I could look up at the verandah from where with almost unbearable suspense we had watched the red-faced British soldiers creep up on their stomachs, rifles at the ready. I could almost feel again the rush of excitement which propelled us into the presence of the nuns to tell them the incredible news. I recognised the eaves under which the hornets had built their nests and had wreaked such terrible retribution on us for our thoughtless interference. I could hear again the haunting sound of scales and arpeggios and that little Italian shepherd boy tune played so beautifully by Lucy, which evoked in me those vague half-recognised longings that music always does.

It was only a few hundred yards to the house occupied by the Danes, but gone were the beautiful flower beds and the paint was peeling badly. I would not be sending my photograph of that to Andy, who would hate to see it all so neglected.

A strong link has now been forged between my mother's family in Burma and mine in England. Burma is going through difficult times and its gentle and dignified people need help in any way we can give them. Rightly or wrongly, I have always felt that my mother was deprived of her two children and finally abandoned. Dying so young (she was not quite thirty) hers was a sad, short life. Perhaps the link forged by my two daughters will now in some way atone for the wrongs done to her. Perhaps one day my twin sons Jasper and Rupert, busy carving a living for themselves, will be the ones to retrace my father's arduous trek from Northern Burma to India, and visit his grave in Calcutta. I have a little idea of the dreadful time he had and of the dangers he had to endure. I have a wish to do my best by both my parents, to understand what they went through rather than judge them, and I hope they will be pleased with my effort to tell their story and my own.

GLOSSARY

aung thu   'winners', a children's team game

ayah   nurse

chatti   cooking pot, food container

chin-lone   ball game

dah   big knife

dhobi   Indian washerman

eingyi   close-fitting jacket or blouse worn with a longyi

gaungbaung   Burmese turbanlike head-dress

gillie dunda   an Indian ball game

Jarruwallah   Indian sweeper

kamauk   Shan broad-brimmed bamboo hat

longyi   Burmese-style sarong

mahadevi   a sawbwa's chief wife

mali   Indian gardener or handyman

maung   younger brother

nat   malign spirit

ngapi   pressed rotten fish dish

phongyi   Burmese monk

phongyi kyaung   monastery

pwè   stage show

shiko   Burmese equivalent of Indian salaam or Japanese kowtow

sawbwa   Shan feudal prince

thakin   master

thankin ma   mistress

thankin ma lé   little mistress

thanahka   a protective facial paste

thayaw   shampoo made from bark of a tree

Thin Gyan   Burmese New Year water festival